Name: _____

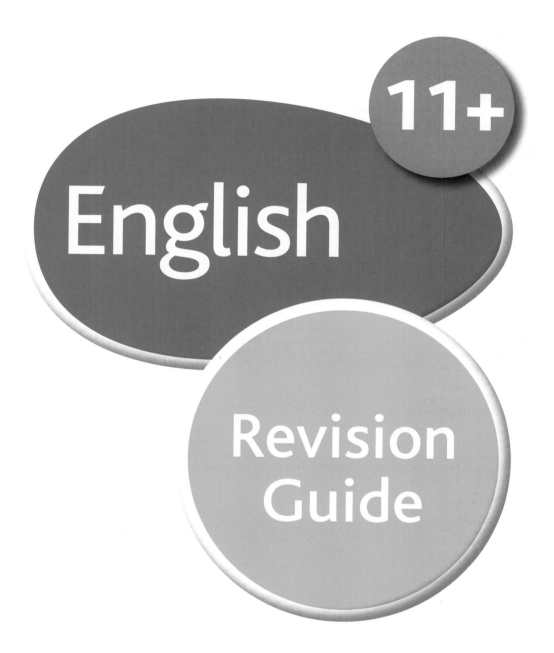

11+

English

Revision Guide

Victoria Burrill

Erika Cross

Jenny Olney

GALORE PARK

AN HACHETTE UK COMPANY

The Publishers would like to thank the following for permission to reproduce copyright material.

Photo credits

p 49 © govicinity - Fotolia; **p 95** *t* © photograph - Fotolia, *b* © Getty Images/Purestock/Thinkstock; **p 96** © Katya Mikhlin - Fotolia; **p 120** © Getty Images/Creatas RF/Thinkstock; **p 121** © Getty Images/iStockphoto/Thinkstock; **p 139** © rudi1976 - Fotolia; **p 140** © okinawakasawa - Fotolia

Acknowledgements

p 46 Henry Wadsworth from 'Rain in Summer'; **p 50** Barack Obama (obtained from www.whitehouse.gov); **p 58** Zizou Corder from *Lionboy* (Puffin Books - permission sought); **p 60** J.R.R. Tolkein from *The Hobbit* (Harper Collins Children's Books - permission sought); **p 61** Charles Lamb from *The Adventures of Ulysses* (CreateSpace Independent Publishing Platform - permission sought); **p 63** Eva Ibbotson from *Journey to the River Sea* (Macmillan Children's Books - permission sought); **p 68** Lauren St John from *Dolphin Song* (Puffin Books - permission sought); **p 71, 72** Diana Wynne Jones from *The Lives of Christopher Chant* (Harper Collins Children's Books); **p 72** Jon Mayhew from *Mortlock* (©Jon Mayhew 2011, "Mortlock", Bloomsbury Publishing Plc.); **p 73** Michael Morpurgo from *Kensuke's Kingdom* (Egmont); **p 74** Alfred Lord Tennyson from 'The Eagle'; **p 75** Michelle Paver from *Wolf Brother* (Orion Children's Books - permission sought); **p 75** Mary Norton from *The Borrowers* (Puffin Books - permission sought); **p 76** Michelle Lovric from *The Mourning Emporium* (Orion Children's Books - permission sought); **p 79** Bill Bryson from *Notes from a Small Island* (Penguin Random House/Harper Collins US - permission sought); **p 82** Samuel Taylor Coleridge from 'The Rime of the Ancient Mariner'; **p 132** Nigel Slater from *Toast: The Story of a Boy's Hunger* (Harper Perennial); **p 137** Barbara Willard from A *Flight of Swans* (Laurel-Leaf - permission sought)

Every effort has been made to trace all copyright holders, but if any have been inadvertently overlooked, the Publishers will be pleased to make the necessary arrangements at the first opportunity.

Although every effort has been made to ensure that website addresses are correct at time of going to press, Galore Park cannot be held responsible for the content of any website mentioned in this book. It is sometimes possible to find a relocated web page by typing in the address of the home page for a website in the URL window of your browser.

Hachette UK's policy is to use papers that are natural, renewable and recyclable products and made from wood grown in sustainable forests. The logging and manufacturing processes are expected to conform to the environmental regulations of the country of origin.

Orders: please contact Bookpoint Ltd, 130 Park Drive, Milton Park, Abingdon, Oxon OX14 4SE. Telephone: (44) 01235 827720. Fax: (44) 01235 400454. Email education@bookpoint.co.uk Lines are open from 9 a.m. to 5 p.m., Monday to Saturday, with a 24-hour message answering service. Visit our website at www.galorepark. co.uk for details of other revision guides for Common Entrance, examination papers and Galore Park publications.

ISBN: 978 1 4718 4922 0

© Victoria Burrill 2016

© Erika Cross, Jenny Olney 2016

First published in 2016

Galore Park Publishing Ltd,

An Hachette UK Company

Carmelite House

50 Victoria Embankment

London EC4Y 0DZ

www.galorepark.co.uk

Impression number   10 9 8 7 6 5 4 3 2 1

Year   2020 2019 2018 2017 2016

Typeset in India

Printed in Spain

Illustrations by Integra Software Services, Ltd.

A catalogue record for this title is available from the British Library.

Contents and progress record

Use this page to plot your revision. Colour in the boxes when you feel confident with the skill and note your score and time for each test in the boxes.

	/ 29	:
	/ 27	:
	/ 23	:

3 Composition

	Revised	Score	Time

How to use this book

Introduction

This book has been written to help you review and develop your skills in English in preparation for your 11+ exam. It will help you to:

- improve your ability to construct clear and appropriate answers
- develop your skills in working with different forms of text
- prepare for writing creatively in a wide range of styles.

The book has been designed to help you develop the necessary skills that you will need to be successful at 11+. Work through the pages with a parent or on your own, then complete the exercises and talk about them afterwards. Use the mark schemes to help you create improved answers. Most topics are covered in two-page sections that can be studied in half an hour. You are more likely to remember important information if you revise in short bursts rather than spending an afternoon when you are tired, so try setting time aside after school two or three days a week, or perhaps at the weekends. You may be surprised at how quickly you progress. Don't be afraid to ask a parent or other adult for help. The book is designed to help you revise – it is not just a series of tests. It is a good opportunity for you to find out what you're really good at already and what you might need a bit more help with.

Pre-Test and the 11+ entrance exams

The Galore Park 11+ series is designed for Pre-Tests and 11+ entrance exams for admission into independent schools. Some exams are similar to those taken in local grammar schools, although most are constructed with an individual school in mind. The weighting of marks in the English tests is divided between writing and comprehension, although spelling, punctuation and grammar is also tested in a range of ways, either directly in questions or indirectly through writing tasks.

Tests are constructed depending on the importance each school places on certain aspects of English, so if you are applying to more than one school you will encounter more than one style of test. These include:

- Pre-Tests delivered on-screen
- 11+ entrance exams in different formats including GL (Granada Learning), CEM (Centre for Evaluation and Monitoring) and ISEB (Independent Schools Examinations Board)
- 11+ entrance exams created specifically for particular independent schools.

Whilst writing a composition is not required in the on-screen Pre-Tests, many schools now use this as a filter and if you are successfully called back to the next stage, you may be given 20–30 minutes for a writing test.

To give you the best chance of success in these assessments, Galore Park has worked with 11+ tutors, independent school teachers, test writers and specialist authors to create this *Revision Guide*.

The content covers the National Curriculum programmes of study for Key Stage 2 as well as the ISEB Common Entrance 11+ syllabus. Some aspects of the Key Stage 3 curriculum are also covered, where this relates to the tests mentioned above.

The Learning Ladders

These ladders appear throughout the book to chart your progress through skills in both writing and comprehension. The book begins by addressing important spelling and punctuation rules then moves up the ladder to review grammar and sentence construction. In Chapter 2 you will focus on comprehension skills (moving up the right hand side of the ladder) and in Chapter 3 you will work on composition skills (moving up the left hand side of the ladder). It is important to remember that comprehension and composition are very closely linked, with many skills that cross over, so you will find a number of connections between the different activities as you complete them.

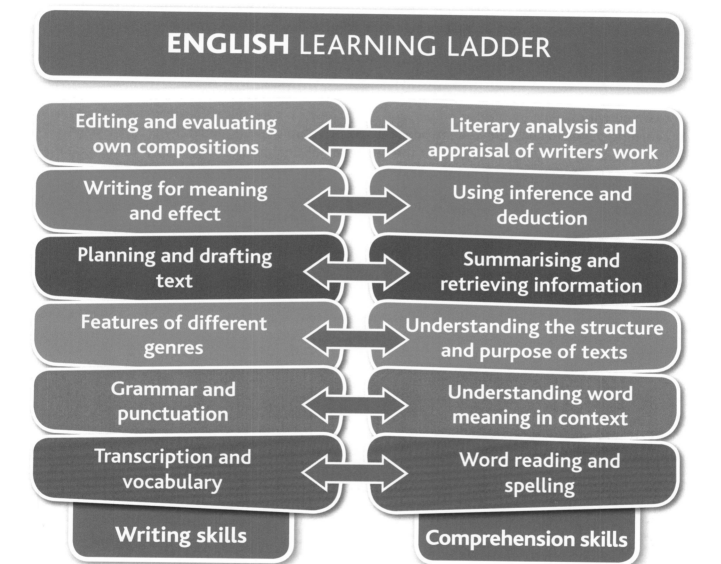

ENGLISH LEARNING LADDER

Editing and evaluating own compositions	Literary analysis and appraisal of writers' work
Writing for meaning and effect	Using inference and deduction
Planning and drafting text	Summarising and retrieving information
Features of different genres	Understanding the structure and purpose of texts
Grammar and punctuation	Understanding word meaning in context
Transcription and vocabulary	Word reading and spelling
Writing skills	Comprehension skills

Working through the book

The **Contents and progress record** helps you to keep track of your progress. When you have finished one of the learning spreads or tests below, turn back to these introductory pages and complete them by:

- colouring in the 'Revised' box on the planner when you are confident you have mastered the skill
- adding in your test scores and time to keep track of how you are getting on and work out which areas you may need more practice in.

The book is divided into four chapters: the first chapter, 'Spelling, punctuation and grammar' refreshes the essential skills you will need to excel in comprehension and writing, covered in the following two chapters. Chapter 4 provides useful information (such as spelling lists and examples of model answers) as well as a glossary of useful words and phrases that appear throughout the book (highlighted in blue).

- **Chapter introductions** explain how the chapter content relates to the 11+ exams. These pages also provide advice for your parents so that they can help you revise with some extra activities.
- **Learning pages** in chapters 1–3 introduce a skill or group of skills, generally across two or four pages ('Identifying text types' at the beginning of Chapter 2 is longer, to provide a clear reference for constructing your own texts later).

Train

Questions to help you revise the skill.

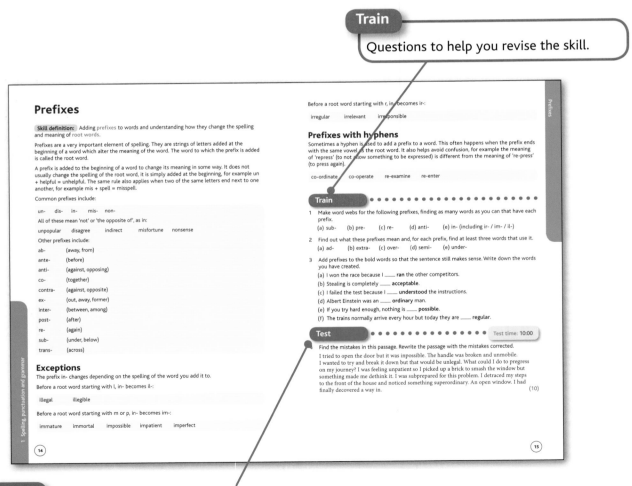

Test

Timed question(s) to see what real exam questions are like. Always complete the questions even if you don't manage them in the time. The practice is important.

- **End of chapter tests** give you a chance to practise more questions relating to the content of the chapter in a short test. The test time given is for an average test (some challenging tests are faster). Always time yourself to build up your speed.
  - Complete the test, aiming for the test time given.
  - Complete the questions you don't finish during the time (but mark down which ones they are).
  - Go through the test again with a friend or parent and talk about the questions and aspects of the writing you found difficult.
- **11+ sample tests** beginning on page 129 are based on challenging 11+ tests to standard timings. The first two tests are multiple-choice. Although the schools you have applied to may not give a separate spelling, punctuation and grammar paper, you are encouraged to complete this test as well as the others to develop your skills in analysis and writing. It is also possible that some similar questions may be introduced into comprehension papers.

  You may find some of the questions hard and find the tests difficult to complete within the time, but don't worry – these are training tests to build up your skills. Agree with your parents on a good time to take each test and set a timer going. Prepare for the test as if you are actually going to sit your 11+ (see 'Test day tips' below).
  - Complete the test with a timer, in a quiet room, noting down how long it takes you.
  - Mark the test using the answers at the back of the book.
  - Go through the test again with a friend or parent and talk about the difficult questions.
  - Have another go at the compositions that you did not choose to give you practice in a variety of writing styles. It is good practice to plan some compositions under timed conditions, even if you don't write the full composition. It helps you to build up a bank of ideas.
  - If you didn't finish the tests in the given time, have another attempt before moving on to more practice tests in the Galore Park *Practice Papers* books.
- **Answers** to all the tests in the book can be found in the cut-out section at the back of the book. Always mark your writing compositions, using the **success grids** beginning on page 141 to help you to understand the features the examiners are looking for. To get a balanced view, try asking a parent to assess your work, then assess it yourself. Use the grids to help you write an improved second draft. You may also find the **model writing samples** on pages 126–128 useful to get a feeling for the standard of answer the examiners are looking for.

  Try not to look at the answers until you have attempted the questions yourself. Most answers have full explanations and a breakdown of marks so you can understand why you might have answered incorrectly.

Test day tips
....
Take time to prepare yourself the day before you go for the test: remember to take enough pens, sharp pencils and an eraser with you. A watch is very important so you can time yourself. Take a bottle of water in with you, if this is allowed, as this will help to keep you hydrated and improves your concentration levels.

... and don't forget to have breakfast before you go!

For parents

This book has been written to help both you and your child prepare for the 11+ entrance exams. It is designed to help you support your child with clear explanations for parents at the beginning of each chapter, which include:

- suggestions on how to support your child through their English revision
- information about how the revision in the chapter relates to the tests
- advice on how additional work can have an impact on success
- activities and games that practice using the skills in enjoyable ways.

The teaching content is designed so that it can be tackled in simple steps. Setting aside time when your child can concentrate fully on short sections when you are there to support them can help to make the experience manageable and enjoyable.

The answers are clearly explained in order to support you and your child in reviewing questions they may have found challenging. Writing is a particularly difficult area to assess and so success grids (see pages 141–144), detailing the points to look for in a well-planned and constructive text, are provided to help you review your child's work. Suggesting that they review their own texts first is a useful exercise in itself as it helps them with their skills in editing and evaluating their own and others' writing. The model writing samples (pages 126–128) are also helpful to illustrate the level of answer expected by the examiners.

As this is a revision guide, the process is as important as the outcome and the most valuable input you can have is discussing the work with your child and helping them to understand the mark schemes and what is expected. Just practising everything independently will not necessarily help your child to develop the necessary skills.

For teachers and tutors

This book has been written for parents and tutors working with children preparing for 11+ entrance exams. Text construction and planning is dealt with in great detail to encourage parents to work with their children to develop these skills. This is felt to be more helpful than a variety of unguided compositions which are difficult to mark. Tutors can select the areas of content they feel most appropriate for the children they are working with in order to consolidate their strengths and improve weaknesses.

Continue your learning journey

When you've completed this *Revision Guide* you can carry on your learning right up until exam day with the following resources.

The Workbooks will further develop your skills with 25 activities (50 smaller activities in *Spelling and Vocabulary*) to work through in each book. To prepare you for the 11+ and Pre-Test exams, these books include more examples of the question variations covered in the practice papers – the more times you practice the questions, the better equipped for the exams you will be!

- *Grammar and Punctuation*: Increase your understanding of grammatical terminology and improve your communication skills.
- *Reading and Comprehension*: Work through comprehension passages and analyse the effective use of language.
- *Spelling and Vocabulary*: Understand the structure and meaning of words and build your vocabulary.
- *Writing*: Experiment with different forms of writing and learn to express your ideas effectively.

Practice Papers 1 and *2* contain twelve model tests replicating different Pre-Test and 11+ exams you may encounter. The papers test your skills in spelling, punctuation and grammar, answering challenging comprehension questions and tackling a variety of writing tasks making sure you are fully prepared for your exams. They also include realistic test timings and fully-explained answers for final test preparation.

① Spelling, punctuation and grammar

Introduction

The aim of this chapter is to revisit and consolidate all of the important elements of spelling, grammar and punctuation that you have probably already learned at school. Many of these skills are best learned through practice and this chapter will give you the opportunity to do that.

The rules on spelling, grammar and punctuation are like the building blocks of language. They lay a foundation for the rest of your writing, and showing an examiner that you are confident with them is important. You may be asked specific questions about them in an exam or you may be judged on your knowledge through your writing or understanding of how an author has written.

While you may already be aware of your own strengths and weaknesses in this area, it is a good idea to revise each element. In an exam, make sure you give yourself an opportunity to show off all of the skills you have. Use speech marks accurately, include an ellipsis, write sentences with clauses in them to show you can use commas. After revising the skills in this chapter, you should feel confident enough to identify and use each language feature.

As you work through this book you will revisit the **learning ladder** shown below. In this chapter you are working through the skills at the bottom of the ladder, and by the end of the book you will have reached the top. In this chapter you are climbing **the first two rungs**. Building a wide vocabulary, increasing your confidence through spelling practice (step 1) and then assembling these words into clear and well-organised writing (step 2) will provide you with the foundations you need to be confident of producing a piece of writing that will make complete sense to the reader. It will also improve your understanding of what you read.

Advice for parents

Spelling, punctuation and grammar have always been an important element of English and have risen in prominence in recent curriculum development. They will be tested in a range of ways, either directly in questions or indirectly through writing tasks. By consolidating knowledge and gaining confidence with these skills, children will be able to devote more attention to the creative process of writing and the deeper understanding of texts which are required in 11+ assessments. These skills and rules will be referred to throughout the rest of this book and so this chapter should be completed first.

It is worth noting that when exam papers are marked by senior schools, more credit will be given to a well-planned, thoughtful and (where appropriate) imaginative piece of writing with some spelling mistakes than one which is technically perfect and dull. It is important to encourage children to use adventurous and meaningful language even if they are not 100 percent sure of a spelling. A balance should be struck. The same goes with grammar – a well-shaped sentence that varies from others but lacks a comma will be valued above a string of simple and plain sentences.

It is always a good idea to encourage your child to check their writing carefully for mistakes in punctuation at least. While it is possible to understand a piece of writing which contains spelling mistakes and the occasional grammatical error, one with little or no punctuation can be very difficult, if not impossible, to comprehend. Therefore, try to get your child to read their writing out loud and 'hear' where the punctuation should go. This, combined with the exercises later in this chapter, should ensure that their writing can be understood.

Learning and practising the rules of spelling, punctuation and grammar can seem rather repetitive and uninspiring to children. The activities in this chapter are designed to make it more exciting and, in addition, you could try out some of the following games and activities together to add to their understanding.

Games

- Word-based board games, for example Scrabble, Boggle, Balderdash, Bananagrams.
- Crosswords and wordsearches (you can complete them from books or create your own).
- Word of the Day – choose a word from the dictionary or an unknown word from a book and challenge the family to use it that day.
- Word Wall – collect new words and difficult spellings using magnetic letters or similar on a fridge or board.
- Word Webs – make webs or spider diagrams of synonyms for common words.
- Writing Rhymes – create rhymes or mnemonics for tricky words.

Reading activities

- Read with your child and discuss spellings.
- Ask questions about punctuation and grammar when reading.
- Keep a word journal, collecting new words and difficult spellings.
- Read a range of text types – newspapers, blogs, letters, non-fiction as well as fiction – to identify different types of SPaG.

Prefixes

Skill definition: Adding prefixes to words and understanding how they change the spelling and meaning of root words.

Prefixes are a very important element of spelling. They are strings of letters added at the beginning of a word which alter the meaning of the word. The word to which the prefix is added is called the root word.

A prefix is added to the beginning of a word to change its meaning in some way. It does not usually change the spelling of the root word, it is simply added at the beginning, for example un + helpful = unhelpful. The same rule also applies when two of the same letters end next to one another, for example mis + spell = misspell.

Common prefixes include:

un-   dis-   in-   mis-   non-

All of these mean 'not' or 'the opposite of', as in:

unpopular   disagree   indirect   misfortune   nonsense

Other prefixes include:

ab-	(away, from)
ante-	(before)
anti-	(against, opposing)
co-	(together)
contra-	(against, opposite)
ex-	(out, away, former)
inter-	(between, among)
post-	(after)
re-	(again)
sub-	(under, below)
trans-	(across)

Exceptions

The prefix in- changes depending on the spelling of the word you add it to.

Before a root word starting with l, in- becomes il-:

illegal   illegible

Before a root word starting with m or p, in- becomes im-:

immature   immortal   impossible   impatient   imperfect

Before a root word starting with r, in- becomes ir-:

irregular   irrelevant   irresponsible

Prefixes with hyphens

Sometimes a hyphen is used to add a prefix to a word. This often happens when the prefix ends with the same vowel as the root word. It also helps avoid confusion, for example the meaning of 'repress' (to not allow something to be expressed) is different from the meaning of 're-press' (to press again).

co-ordinate   co-operate   re-examine   re-enter

Train

1 Make word webs for the following prefixes, finding as many words as you can that have each prefix.

(a) sub-   (b) pre-   (c) re-   (d) anti-   (e) in- (including ir- / im- / il-)

2 Find out what these prefixes mean and, for each prefix, find at least three words that use it.

(a) ad-   (b) extra-   (c) over-   (d) semi-   (e) under-

3 Add prefixes to the bold words so that the sentence still makes sense. Write down the words you have created.

(a) I won the race because I ____ **ran** the other competitors.

(b) Stealing is completely ____ **acceptable**.

(c) I failed the test because I ____ **understood** the instructions.

(d) Albert Einstein was an ____ **ordinary** man.

(e) If you try hard enough, nothing is ____ **possible**.

(f) The trains normally arrive every hour but today they are ____ **regular**.

Test

Test time: 10:00

4 Find the mistakes in this passage. Rewrite the passage with the mistakes corrected.

I tried to open the door but it was inpossible. The handle was broken and unmobile. I wanted to try and break it down but that would be unlegal. What could I do to pregress on my journey? I was feeling unpatient so I picked up a brick to smash the window but something made me dethink it. I was subprepared for this problem. I detraced my steps to the front of the house and noticed something superordinary. An open window. I had finally decovered a way in.

(10)

Suffixes

Skill definition: Adding **suffixes** to words and understanding how they change the spelling and meaning of root words.

Suffixes are another very important element of spelling. They are strings of letters added at the end of a word which alter the meaning of a word. The word to which the suffix is added is called the root word.

Suffixes can be added to different types of words. Some examples are shown below:

Verbs

-ing	(happening now – sing/singing)
-ed	(in the past – walk/walked)
-ment	(changes a verb into an abstract noun – agree/agreement)
-able	(changes a verb into an adjective meaning 'able to be' – bear/bearable)
-ible	(changes a verb into an adjective meaning 'able to be' – convert/convertible)
-ion	(changes a verb into a noun – invent/invention)
-ation	(changes a verb into a noun – sense/sensation)

Nouns

-less	(changes a noun into an adjective meaning 'none or without' – hope/hopeless)
-ful	(changes a noun into an adjective meaning 'with'– doubt/doubtful)
-ous	(changes a noun into an adjective – poison/poisonous)

Adjectives

-ness	(changes an adjective into a noun – happy/happiness)
-ly	(changes an adjective to an adverb – quick/quickly)
-er	(changes an adjective into a comparative – slow/slower)
-est	(changes an adjective into a superlative – smart/smartest)
-en	(changes an adjective into a verb – flat/flatten)

> *One suffix that is commonly misspelled is -ful. The only time you write 'full' (with double 'll') is when the word is used on its own, as in 'The bag is full to the brim.' Otherwise, there is just one 'l', as in useful, beautiful, handful, spoonful, etc.*

There are many rules for adding suffixes. Here are some general rules.

● If the last (or only) syllable of a word is emphasised and ends with one consonant which has just one vowel before it, the final consonant is doubled before any ending beginning with a vowel is added.

forget – forgetting/forgettable   clap – clapping/clapped

● If the last syllable is not emphasised, do not double the consonant.

garden – gardening   limit – limiting/limited

Train

1   Following the last two rules, add -ed and -ing to the root words below. Write down the words you have created.

(a) slip   (b) trip   (c) tap   (d) pardon   (e) clip

● When adding a suffix to a word ending in y with a consonant before it, change the y to an i before adding the suffix.

fury – furious   happy – happiness   funny – funniest

● If there is a vowel before the y then do not change the y to an i.

play – playing/played   grey – greying/greyest

● Exception: adding -ing to verbs.

trying   frying   crying

Train

2   Following the rules above, find the incorrectly spelled words and write them correctly.

frayed   betraied   smellyest   gloomily   muddyest   repling
displayed   bulkier   curlyest   juicyness   cheeriness

● A single e at the end of the root word is dropped before -ing, -ed, -er, -est, -y or any other suffix beginning with a vowel.

hike – hiking/hiked   shine – shining/shiny   define – defining/defined/definable

● There is an exception: being.

Train

3   Add the appropriate suffixes, -ing and -ed, or -er and -est, to the following root words. Write down the words you have created.

(a) accelerate   (b) assume   (c) exclude   (d) fine
(e) strange   (f) gentle   (g) simple

● When adding -ing, -ed, -er, -est and -y to words of one syllable ending in a single consonant with a single vowel before the consonant, the last consonant must be doubled if the vowel sound is to be kept 'short'.

pat – patting/patted   flat – flatter/flatten/flattest

● There is an exception: the letter x is never doubled.

4 Find the mistakes in this passage. Write out the passage with the mistakes corrected.

It was the hotest day on record and Jane had stoped skiping in the park because she was sweatty and thirsty. She floped onto the grass and siped on her water. She felt sleeppy so closed her droopy eyelids and dozzed off. When she awoke, her eyes gradually fixxed on the figure standing before her.

● If a suffix starts with a consonant, the root word does not change unless the word ends in a y.

| fulfil – fulfilment | great – greatness | hope – hopeful | beauty – beautiful |

● There is an exception: argument

5 Add -ment or -ness onto these words. Write down the words you have created.

(a) happy   **(b)** govern   **(c)** ill   **(d)** amuse   **(e)** improve

(f) fit   **(g)** foolish   **(h)** heavy   **(i)** sad   **(j)** lonely

Some suffixes have their own rules, which have to be learned.

The -ous suffix

● Sometimes the root word is obvious and the usual rules apply for adding suffixes beginning with vowels.

danger – dangerous   fame – famous

● Sometimes there is no obvious root word.

tremendous   jealous   enormous

● -our is changed to -or before -ous is added.

glamour – glamorous

● The final e of the root word must be kept if the -dg sound of g is to be kept.

courage – courageous

● If there is a short i sound before the -ous ending, it is usually spelled as i.

curious   obvious

● A few words are spelled with an e not an i.

hideous   spontaneous

Train

6   Follow the rules to correct these mistakes. Write down the corrected sentences.

   (a) Varyous people have climbed the mountaineous regions of Nepal.

   (b) The comedian was very humourous.

   (c) The cost of the holiday was outragous.

The -ly suffix

● The suffix -ly changes an adjective to an adverb. The rules stated earlier still apply. The suffix -ly starts with a consonant, so it is added straight on to most root words.

   large – largely   wide – widely

● If the root word ends in y and has more than one syllable, change the y to an i.

   angry – angrily   grumpy – grumpily

● If the root word ends with -le, the -le changes to -ly.

   gently   simply

● If the root word ends with -ic, add -ally instead of -ly,

   basically   frantically   dramatically

● There are exceptions: publicly, truly, duly, wholly.

Train

7   Add an -ly word to these sentences. Write out the completed sentences.

   (a) The pianist played _____ .

   (b) Every evening I _____ complete my homework.

   (c) This year my exam results were _____ better than last year.

   (d) _____ it is nearly time to go to school.

Test   Test time: 10:00

8   Find the mistakes in this passage. Write out the corrected passage.

   Suddenly, the ship swaied from side to side, battleing the enormous waves. The couragous captain controled the sails and the crew rallied together to bail out the water. The choppy-ness of the water worsened and the boat tiped over dangerusly. There was no merryment aboard that day. Everyone franticaly worked to survive.   (10)

Plurals and silent letters

Skill definition: Creating plural nouns using a range of spelling rules and identifying words that have silent letters and unstressed vowels.

Plurals, meaning more than one of something, are used in almost every piece of writing and mostly follow a number of standard rules. However there are several exceptions that must also be learned. It is equally important to know when silent letters are used as they are not heard or pronounced, making the words harder to spell.

Plurals

Plural means more than one of something. There are several rules for making nouns plural.

● Usually we add -s.

table – tables   dog – dogs

● If a word ends in s, x, z, ch or sh, add -es.

class – classes   fox – foxes   batch – batches   wish – wishes

● If a word ends in y after a consonant, replace the i with y and add -ies. If a word ends in a y after a vowel, just add s.

baby – babies   donkey – donkeys

● Change a single f at the end of a word to v and add es.

calf – calves   but   roof – roofs

● Add -es to most words ending in o (apart from musical words, foreign words or shortened words).

buffalo – buffaloes   piano – pianos   avocado – avocados   hippo – hippos

● Words with a Greek or Latin origin have other rules.

-is changes to -es	-um changes to -a	-on changes to -a
analysis – analyses	curriculum – curricula	phenomenon – phenomena
-us changes to -i	-a changes to -ae	-ex changes to -ices
focus – foci	antenna – antennae	index – indices

● There are some complete exceptions.

child – children   person – people

● Some words don't change at all in the plural.

sheep   aircraft   offspring   salmon

Train

1 (a) Make a list of ten unusual plurals or exceptions to the rules. Keep the list safe and add to it when you come across new examples.

   (b) Some words, such as 'cattle', only exist in the plural. Can you find any more of these words?

Silent letters and unstressed vowels

Silent letters are letters we cannot hear when saying a word, but which we must include when writing it.

- A silent b sometimes occurs after m, as in lam**b**, bom**b** and thum**b**, and before t, as in de**b**t.
- A silent g or k sometimes occurs before n, as in **g**nome, **k**nee and **k**nife.
- A silent w often occurs before r as in **w**restle, **w**rist and **w**rap.
- A silent p sometimes occurs before n, s or t, as in **p**neumatic, **p**sychiatry and **p**terodactyl.
- There is sometimes a silent t in the middle of a word, as in bus**t**le and lis**t**en.
- A silent n is sometimes found at the end of a word, as in hym**n**, autum**n** and colum**n**.
- A silent c may occur after an s, as in s**c**ience, s**c**ene and mus**c**le.

You will also come across some unstressed vowels, which are vowels that cannot be heard in the normal pronunciation of a word.

a – sep**a**rate   e – fright**e**ning   i – parl**i**ament

Train

2 Identify the unstressed vowel or silent letter in these words. Look up the meaning of the words that you don't recognise.

(a) desperate   (b) generous   (c) interesting   (d) jewellery

(e) subtle   (f) knowledgeable   (g) soften   (h) answer

(i) wrangle   (j) knead   (k) mortgage

Test

Test time: 15:00

3 Rewrite the following passage, correcting the spelling errors:

Arthur was out joging one morning. As he ran he took in the senery and found himself growing envyous of the beautiful houses and gardens he passed along his route. He looked at his watch. His face was solem when he realised that his time was slower than the day before. Dissappointed, he hasened to make up the lost time by sprinting for the next five hundred metres but he suddenly felt an agonising pain in his left gnee. As he hobbled towards the park he saw a small dog exploreing the undergrowth. It seemed unatural for a dog to be in the park without an owner in sight at this our of the day.   (10)

Homophones, homonyms and other commonly confused words

Skill definition: Distinguishing between homophones/homonyms and other words that are often confused.

The English language has many words that sound and look similar. However, they do not always have the same or even a similar meaning. It is important to recognise which is which and to understand the difference.

Homophones

Words that *sound the same* but are *spelled differently* and have different meanings are called homophones (*homos* = same and *phon* = sound). There are hundreds of these words in English that we use on a daily basis. When you are writing, it is very easy to make mistakes with homophones and using the wrong homophone can make your writing appear careless. Some homophones to learn are:

whose / who's	Whose is this? / Who's at the door?
to / too / two	Shall we go to the shop? / Can I come too? / I will buy two sweets.
there / their / they're	There is the boy. / Their shoes are dirty. / They're going to the seaside.

Train ●

1   Find a homophone for each of these words. Write down the meaning of both words.

   (a) morning   **(b)** principal   **(c)** passed   **(d)** allowed

   (e) alter   **(f)** compliment   **(g)** hole

   See how many more you can come up with.

Homonyms

Homonyms (*homos* = same and *nym* = name) are words that are *spelled the same* and *sound the same* but have different meanings. These include words such as:

bark (the noise a dog makes)	bark (the rough outside of a tree)
fine (money paid for a misdemeanour)	fine (pretty good)
fan (an enthusiastic supporter)	fan (a device for cooling something down)

There are hundreds of common homonyms and you will need to use the context of the text you are reading to work out the meaning.

Train ●

2   Write down as many meanings as you can for each of these homonyms. For each homonym, challenge yourself by writing a sentence in which the homonym appears more than once, but with different meanings.

(a) long   (b) back   (c) match   (d) left

(e) right   (f) leaves   (g) rose

Confusable words

There are lots of other words that many people often get confused. Unfortunately there is no magic way of telling these apart. You just have to learn the spellings and their definitions so you know which one to use in the sentence you are writing. The list below is a good place to start. Use this to begin your own list of commonly confused words and add any new ones that you discover.

Accept means 'to take willingly'	The boy got up on stage to **accept** his trophy.
Except means 'excluding'	Everyone was invited to the party **except** me.
Affect means 'to influence/change'	The weather **affects** my mood.
Effect means 'a change/consequence'	The weather had a dramatic **effect** on our holiday.
Loose means 'not tight'	Since my diet, my trousers seem **loose**.
Lose means 'to misplace'	I often **lose** my car keys.

With some of these words, the ending will help. In the following examples, -ce and -cy endings indicate nouns and -se and -sy endings indicate verbs.

advice / advise   device / devise   licence / license
practice / practise   prophecy / prophesy

Train •

3   Write a definition for each of the following pairs of commonly confused words and then use each word correctly in a sentence:

(a) dairy / diary   (b) stationery / stationary

(c) precede / proceed   (d) licence / license

Test • • • • • • • • • • • • • • • • • •   Test time: 20:00

4   Rewrite the following text, correcting the spelling errors.

Once their was a bare who lived in the woods. He was a very grumpy bear because he had tripped over a lose rock and know he had a saw toe. The plaster he had used had stuck too his fir. To make himself feel better he maid a sandwich but his foot was still hurting so he decided to phone the doctor. The receptionist told him he wood have to weight a weak four an appointment when the doctor would be able to advice him on what to do. When he herd this the bear could not except that he would have to bee patient. He didn't no weather to scream allowed or grown quietly. "Grate," he growled as he slammed down the phone. The only thing he could think to do now was eat sum desert to cheer himself up before it was passed his bedtime.   (24)

Basic punctuation

Skill definition: Understanding the functions of basic punctuation marks and their use in sentences.

Punctuation is an essential part of writing. Without it, much of what we write would not make sense. Look at these sentences:

Most of the time-travellers worry about their luggage.

Most of the time, travellers worry about their luggage.

The actual words are the same, but the meaning is different. The first sentence means that the majority of people who travel through time worry about their luggage, and sounds like a line from science fiction. The second suggests that usually when people travel they worry about their luggage, and sounds like a newspaper or magazine report.

As these examples show, punctuation does not just stop us writing nonsense, it also makes a difference to the real meaning of a sentence.

Full stops

The full stop is the most important punctuation mark of all. It is used to divide your writing into sentences.

Sentences are the building blocks used to construct a passage of text. They come in all lengths, but however long or short a sentence is, it must contain at least one complete fact. 'Up the mountain' is not a sentence because we do not know who or what is going (or lives) up the mountain. 'Adam is climbing up the mountain' is a sentence because it is complete.

Another way of looking at it is that a sentence has to have a subject (someone or something, in this case 'Adam') and a verb (an action, in this case 'climbing'). Sentences always start with a capital letter and end with a full stop, exclamation mark or question mark.

Capital letters

As well as using a capital letter at the beginning of a sentence, you also use them for the following:

- Names of people (e.g. Miss Grace Langley, Mr Kevin Bright, Queen Elizabeth)
- Titles of books, films, plays, TV programmes (e.g. *The Twits, Toy Story, King Lear, Doctor Who*)
- Names of places, including towns, countries, mountains, rivers and famous buildings (e.g. Leeds, Scotland, River Stour, Victoria and Albert Museum)
- Days, months of the year, festivals, special holidays (e.g. Monday, December, Easter Sunday, Ramadan)
- Names of companies and brands (e.g. Nike, Tesco, Microsoft)
- Acronyms (e.g. UNESCO, NATO)

Train

1 Rewrite the passage below, adding in the missing full stops and capital letters.

punctuation is very important to writers it helps them to divide their writing into sentences and to ensure that what they want to say is clear and can be understood the writing of authors such as charles dickens and william shakespeare would be impossible to understand without punctuation their stories have been translated into many languages including french and russian and these languages also use punctuation without it we would be very confused

Question marks (?) and exclamation marks (!)

Use a question mark when a question is being asked (Are we there yet?) and an exclamation mark if you want to make what someone says sound dramatic, show emotion or give a command (Good grief! That's revolting! Pick that up!)

Do not over-use exclamation marks. If your choice of words is good enough then they will not be necessary. And when you do use them, use only one!

Train

2 Look at the sentences below and decide whether they need a question mark or exclamation mark or neither. Rewrite them, correcting any mistakes you find.

(a) who is responsible for protecting our environment

(b) hurry up

(c) what a fantastic result

(d) are you sure you want to go to james' house

(e) i wondered if i should stay at home or go to the party

Test   Test time: 15:00

3 Rewrite this passage, adding in the missing punctuation:

kaya could see exotic fruits and vegetables on every market stall the smells were enticing and her stomach began to rumble what an amazing sight she could not quite believe that planet earth could produce so much incredible produce what should she try first she was so excited to be in brazil and could not wait to experience all it had to offer where to begin   (16)

Commas and apostrophes

Skill definition: Identifying and using commas accurately in sentences, and using **apostrophes** for both **contraction** and possession.

Both commas and apostrophes are vital for clarity in writing but are often used incorrectly. It is important to understand where they should be used and how to use them correctly.

Commas

Commas are used in a variety of ways.

● Commas are used to separate items in a list.
  The list can be of single words:

He did his work quietly, neatly, thoroughly and efficiently.

She drove a fast, red, sporty car.

  or the list can be of **phrases**:

He weeded the garden, put out the rubbish, cooked the supper and then sat down for a rest.

Spanish is spoken in Spain, in parts of South America and on some islands around the world.

  or it can be a list of simple sentences:

I enjoy swimming, my sister likes football and my brother prefers hockey.

The sun shone, the food was delicious and the views were spectacular.

The last two items in a list of phrases should be separated with the word 'and' rather than another comma.

● When we write a person's name or refer to them in some other way, the phrase containing this information is separated from the rest of the sentence by a comma (or sometimes two). For example:

Welcome, my friends, to my birthday party.

Finlay, will you help me with my homework?

Do not do that, you fool!

● Commas are used to separate extra information from the main sentence. For example:

My friend Megan, who is in Year 5, has just won a writing competition.

Leonardo da Vinci, the famous painter and inventor, was born in the fifteenth century.

Train

1   Make a list to answer the following questions. Make your list into a full sentence.

(a) Name five jobs you would like to do when you are older.

(b) List five things you would like for your birthday.

(c) Think of five adjectives to describe yourself.

2   Add a phrase or clause to the beginning or end of these sentences using a comma to separate it.

(a) Amar went to the cinema.   (b) We smiled and laughed.

(c) Rosie and Yasmin sang a duet.   (d) I would like to learn to swim.

3   Add a clause into the middle of these sentences.

(a) Alfie passed his violin exam.   (b) The thief sprinted across the road.

Apostrophes

Apostrophes are used in two ways:

● To show that a letter or letters have been missed out of a word to shorten it (contraction). The apostrophe shows where the letter or letters have been removed. This should help you spell these words.

do not – don't   would not – wouldn't

I will – I'll   he had – he'd   we have – we've

> *It's* means 'it is', e.g. It's raining hard outside.
>
> *Its* means 'belonging to it', e.g. The cat was chasing its tail.

● To show that something or someone owns something (possession).
If an article belongs to one person or thing, an apostrophe followed by an s is added to the word. For example:

the cat's whiskers – the whiskers belonging to the cat

my neighbour's car – the car belonging to my neighbour

If the article belongs to more than one person or thing and it ends in an s, just an apostrophe is added. For example:

the cats' whiskers – the whiskers belonging to two or more cats

my neighbours' cars – the cars belonging to two or more of my neighbours

If the plural does not end in an s, add an apostrophe followed by an s. For example:

the children's books – the books belonging to the children

the people's opinions – the opinions belonging to the people

> If you are using someone's name and it ends in s, just add an apostrophe. For example, Charles' house or Jess' bike.

4   Rewrite the following passage, adding in the missing apostrophes.

I wont be able to go Sams party. Hell be twelve years old on Thursday. Ill be sad to miss it because his mums cooking is always delicious. The cakes icing is soft and the pizzas crust is crispy. The drinks are always fizzy and his brother James plays good music. James speakers are really loud!

Test • • • • • • • • • • • • • • • • • • •   Test time: 10:00

5   Why are commas used in this sentence?

'At the weekend I went swimming, visited a museum, played football in the garden and completed my homework.'   (1)

6   Explain why the author has used commas in the following sentence.

'Janie, who was exhausted after climbing to the top of the hill, slumped down onto the grass and took a long drink of water.'   (1)

7   Add the missing commas to this passage.   (5)

Chris who was revising for his exams made a timetable for his bedroom wall. It showed which subjects he had to revise when he had time to revise and which books he would need to use. He was organised efficient enthusiastic and his dad was proud of all the hard work he was putting in.

8   What is the purpose of the apostrophe in the following sentence?

'We looked everywhere but we could not find the boys' coats.'   (1)

9   How are the two apostrophes in this sentence used differently?

'It's time to go to Sarah's party.'   (2)

10   Add the missing apostrophes to this passage.   (5)

Carolyns favourite place to visit is the zoo. She loves to see the monkeys jumping around their trees and the elephants huge trunks spraying water. She always visits when the penguins are being fed so that she can see the other peoples reactions. Shes also a fan of the aquarium and its multicoloured fish but she doesnt like the reptile house. The snakes beady eyes are a bit frightening.

Parentheses

Skill definition: Using different forms of parenthesis to separate information from the main sentence.

Using parenthesis is a good way to add detail and depth to writing. Parenthesis is a term for any kind of phrase that can be removed from a sentence without altering the meaning. Brackets are often used in **non-fiction writing**. Commas and dashes can do exactly the same job and can help to build complex sentences. These are more usually seen in **narrative writing**.

It is important to know which type of parenthesis to use in a particular style of writing. Dashes mark more of a break than commas.

The cat, whose hair stood up on end in fright, leapt easily over the dilapidated fence.

The boat – a tall and rickety craft – tentatively set sail as the clouds rolled in.

Brackets are often (but not only) used in formal or technical writing.

Carbon (one of the most common elements on the Earth) is vital for life.

The information in the parentheses is usually less important than the main part of the sentence. It is interesting information or adds clarification, but the sentence should make sense without it.

Train •

1 For each of the following phrases, write a sentence including the phrase in parentheses. You need to decide whether to use commas, dashes or brackets.

(a) who was tall and skinny like a lamppost

(b) the largest city in England

(c) the only witness to the crime

Test • • • • • • • • • • • • • • • • • Test time: 05:00

2 Rewrite this passage, adding in parentheses where required:

Cats which are one of the most popular pets in this country are friendly and lovable companions. Most people over 75 per cent according to a study would like to have a pet. Different breeds offer different benefits. Some stay indoors such as Persians and others such as Ragdolls like to adventure outdoors. Everyone in the family both young and old will enjoy having a feline companion.

(10)

Punctuating speech

Speech marks

Skill definition: Punctuating speech accurately.

When writing narrative, **dialogue** is an effective technique to use. It needs to be punctuated accurately in order for the meaning to be clear. Without speech punctuation, a story would become extremely hard to understand.

When reading a comic, it is very easy to see who is speaking and what they are saying because each character's words are written in speech bubbles. In writing, the actual words spoken are placed inside speech marks to keep them separate from the rest of the sentence. For example:

"What are you doing?" asked Mr Edwards.

Note here that the question mark is inside the speech marks because it is part of what Mr Edwards has said.

"What," asked Mr Edwards, "are you doing?"

When the words being spoken are split, commas are used to separate the speech and the narration. The first comma is inside the speech marks because it indicates a break in the speech. The second is outside the speech marks because it shows a break in the narration.

Mr Edwards asked, "What are you doing?"

In this example where the narration comes first, a comma is used before the speech marks to show a pause between the narration and the speech. The pause is not part of the speech so it is outside the speech marks.

The only time when you do not need to use speech marks to show that someone is speaking is in a play script. This is because, in a play, all the words are spoken so the clarification that speech marks give is not necessary.

Jack:	Quick, let's go!
Alicia:	But where? We're trapped!
Jack:	Over here, the window's open a crack. We can prise it open.
Alicia:	Are you sure?
Jack:	Yes, but we have to do it immediately. I can hear footsteps in the corridor.

The character names on the left show who is speaking. As the rest of the script is all dialogue, there is no need for speech marks.

To make it even clearer who is speaking, always start a new line when a new person begins talking. This is called 'new speaker, new line'.

Sometimes you will need to use two lots of speech marks when there is a quotation within some speech. Use double speech marks for the main speech and single quotation marks for the quotation within the speech. For example:

This evening Mum said to me, "Your head teacher called and said, 'Sam has won the creative writing competition this year,' and I almost cried with happiness."

The double speech marks show Mum's words as she is the actual speaker. The single speech marks show that she is repeating someone else's words. A comma is used before and after the repeated words following the normal rules of speech punctuation.

Train

1   Rewrite this passage, adding in the missing speech marks. Remember to start a new line when a new person starts speaking.

It was the night before my sister's birthday and Mum and I were in the kitchen, frantically baking a cake. Get me the butter from the fridge screamed Mum in a panic. I can't find it I replied which shelf is it on. I don't know. Use your eyes she retorted. Finally I found it and gave it to Mum. Just as I did she knocked the flour off the counter and all over the floor. Look what you've done now she yelled. She was covered in flour from head to toe. There was silence for a minute then we both burst out laughing. Would it be better to buy a cake at the supermarket asked Mum.

Test

Test time: 05:00

For each line of this passage, identify which part has a mistake in it by writing down the correct letter. If there is no mistake, write N for 'None'. Each question is one mark.

2   Go to your room shouted Mum. It felt like she was furious again.
      A   B   C   D   E N

3   I was constantly in trouble these days. "Now" echoed her voice up the stairs.
      A   B   C   D   E   N

4   I slowly trudged upstairs. "It's not fair. I haven't done anything
      A   B   C   D   E N

5   I muttered to myself. I could hear Mum still clattering about in the kitchen.
      A   B   C   D   E   N

6   I turned the radio up loud to drown out the noise. Turn it down came the voice from downstairs.
      A   B   C   D   E   N

Colons, semicolons and ellipses

Skill definition: Using colons and semicolons accurately.

Colons and semicolons are often avoided as they are thought to be hard to use. In actual fact they can really add to the meaning of a sentence and show an examiner that you know how to use the full range of punctuation.

Colons

A colon (:) is often used to introduce a list. Commas are used to separate the items in the list.

I bought the ingredients: flour, eggs, sugar, butter, dried fruit and vanilla essence.

Colons can also be used between two parts of a sentence when the second illustrates or explains the first. As the two parts are related, no capital letter is needed after the colon.

He got what he wished for: a brand new bike.

Honesty is the best policy: nobody trusts a liar.

Some of the best painters in history were Italian: Leonardo da Vinci and Michelangelo, to name just two.

Note that capital letters are *not* used after the colon unless the first word is a proper noun, as in the last example.

Colons are also used in play scripts. They go after the character's name and before the words that the character says. In the example below, the text spoken is a sentence so does begin with a capital letter.

Hamlet: To be, or not to be, that is the question.

When items are being listed on individual lines, a colon can be used to introduce the list.

Our school values are:

● honesty
● respect
● enthusiasm
● teamwork
● kindness

Train

1   Rewrite these sentences, adding in the missing colons.

   (a) He wrote a short list for Santa a red bike, a new pencil case and a book about dinosaurs.

   (b) He couldn't answer the teacher he had completely forgotten the question.

   (c) For the exam you will need the following items a black pen, a 30 cm ruler, a sharp pencil and an eraser.

   (d) His hard work paid off the concert was a success.

   (e) The head teacher made an announcement the netball match was cancelled.

Semicolons

A semicolon (;) is used between two clauses in a sentence. It makes a stronger pause in a sentence than a comma, but not as strong a pause as a full stop. If you use a semicolon, be sure to check that each group of words either side of it makes sense on its own. For example:

> She studied English at university; she wants to be an author.

Train

2   Rewrite these sentences, adding a semicolon and a second clause to each.

(a) Exercising is important.

(b) It is not easy to learn to drive.

(c) Books make wonderful presents.

Ellipses

An ellipsis (...) is a series of three dots used to mark a missing word, phrase or sentence in a piece of writing. Ellipses are used to show an unfinished or interrupted thought or idea. They are a good way to punctuate a cliffhanger or build tension. For example:

> The door swung open and she cautiously peered inside. It was too dark to see at first but as her eyes adjusted to the light it suddenly became clear ...

An ellipsis can also be used to show a pause or hesitation.

> "I don't know ... I can't remember," she murmured.

Train

3   Write the opening paragraph of a story about a haunted house using ellipses to show the character is frightened and to build tension for the reader.

Test

Test time: 05:00

4   Rewrite this paragraph, correcting the punctuation errors:

Sam was happy he had finally finished his homework. He had piles of it this weekend French Science Maths Geography and History. It seemed unfair. His brother didn't have any homework he was playing on his laptop. His sister didn't have any homework she was playing outside on the swings. Being the oldest was tough but he hoped all the hard work would pay off. Eventually

(8)

Types of sentence and clauses

Skill definition: Demonstrating competence with syntax and using relative clauses.

Whether you are reading or writing, it is important to be aware of how sentences are constructed and the effect that has for the reader.

There are three main types of sentences: simple, compound and complex.

The type of sentence used can affect the mood or pace of a piece of writing. You should use short, simple sentences when you want to speed up the action or add excitement.

Compound and complex sentences help to add detail at the beginning of a story, or when introducing new characters.

Simple sentences

When you first started writing, these were the sentences you used. Simple sentences contain one idea each. For example:

My name is Simon.

The sunflower grew quickly.

The car sped down the road.

Compound sentences

Once you mastered simple sentences, you joined some of them together with a conjunction (such as 'and', 'but', 'for', 'so', 'then') to make compound sentences. For example:

My name is Simon **and** I am six years old.

The sunflower grew quickly **until** it was two metres tall **and** it towered over me.

Train ●

1   Write five pairs of simple sentences, for example: 'Michael likes broccoli'. 'James likes peas'. Then turn each pair into a compound sentence, by adding a conjunction, for example: 'Michael likes broccoli but James likes peas'.

Complex sentences

A complex sentence is formed from two or more groups of words. One group of words will make sense on its own (we call this the main clause) and the other does not make sense on its own (this is the subordinate clause). The job of the subordinate clause is to add more detail to the main clause; it can be at the beginning, middle or end of the sentence. It should be separated from the rest of the sentence by a comma.

Here are three complex sentences with the subordinate clauses underlined:

Although I was scared, I went to the dentist.

The cat, while trying to escape from the dog, ran up the tree.

I finished my homework, even though I needed some help.

Clauses that begin with *who, whom, whose, which, where, when* or *that* are known as **relative clauses**. They work like adjectives because they tell the reader more about the noun. For example:

I sprinted to the finish line, which was only a few metres away.

Train ●

2   Read each of the following complex sentences and identify the subordinate clause.

(a) Lucinda, who was an excellent gymnast, won three medals in yesterday's competition.

(b) As it was raining, I took my umbrella.

(c) The schoolchildren ran across the playground, as they laughed their heads off.

3   Use these subordinate clauses to write your own complex sentences.

(a) which tasted delicious

(b) while I was waiting for the train

(c) although he was still grinning

4   Write some complex sentences using *who, whom, whose, which, where* and *when* to make relative clauses, for example: 'I wrote a letter to my friend *who had moved to Australia*'.

> It is important to remember to use a mixture of sentence types in your writing, and to use them correctly. You would not, for example, use complex sentences when writing a set of instructions. Short, simple sentences would be better because they are easier for people to follow.

Test ●   Test time: 08:00

5   Rewrite the following passage using a mixture of simple, compound and complex sentences to make it sound more interesting. You may wish to change the wording slightly, but make sure that you do not lose any of the meaning.

My sister is called Maisie. She is four. She likes dancing and swimming. Sometimes she annoys me. She takes my toys without asking. Her best friend is called Freya. Freya lives next door. They like to play on the trampoline in our garden. The trampoline is huge. Maisie and Freya make lots of noise. They love playing together. I wish I had a brother. We could play with dinosaurs. Maisie does not like dinosaurs. She says they are silly. I don't think they are silly. I like them.

(10)

Parts of speech

Skill definition: Recognising the terminology for different types of words and identifying each element in a sentence.

It is important to know the vocabulary associated with the parts of speech. You may be asked to identify a particular type of word in an exam or to comment on the use of verbs or adjectives in a text. Use the information below to revise the parts of speech.

	Definition	Example
Nouns	Things or items	table, pencil, idea, cloud
Proper nouns	Nouns that are names of people, places, nationalities, months, etc. (They are always capitalised.)	Sarah, Germany, Spanish, Thursday, Cadbury
Abstract nouns	Nouns that can't be touched or seen	determination, courage, hindsight
Verbs	Action words	to run, to think, to jump, to agree
Adjectives	Describing words	long, difficult, smooth, clever
Adverbs	Words that modify or describe an action word	carefully, quickly, immediately, suddenly
Pronouns	Replacements for nouns to avoid repetition	her, him, we, it, me
Prepositions	Words showing direction or position	to, from, under, towards
Conjunctions (sometimes called connectives)	Joining words used in compound sentences	and, but, although
Interjections	Words used to express emotion or a pause	erm, yikes, gosh, hooray, wow

Some words fall into more than one category. For example, 'back' can be a verb, an adjective and a noun.

He had to **back** the car out of the car park.

We all sat in the **back** row.

Gemma hurt her **back**.

It is important to recognise which category of word is being used to help you understand a text.

Here are some other words that fall into more than one part of speech.

	Verb	Adjective/adverb	Noun
well	His eyes welled up with tears.	I played the piano very well.	She dropped the bucket down the well.
round	The dog rounded up the sheep.	The food was on a round plate.	I made the final round of the competition.
right	We righted the boat when it capsized.	The answer was right.	We all have rights and responsibilities.
light	We always light candles during a power cut.	Let's paint the walls light blue.	I switched on the light.

Train

1   Rewrite these sentences, adding some adjectives and adverbs.

(a) The dog ran across the park and started to dig under the tree.

(b) The ship glided over the water with the wind in its sails.

(c) The car drove through the town and parked outside the house.

2   Rewrite these sentences, adding appropriate prepositions and conjunctions in the gaps.

(a) Dad went _____ the supermarket _____ we had run out of milk.

(b) I found my slippers _____ the sofa _____ it was the last place I looked.

(c) I heard the car coming _____ me _____ I waited before I crossed the road.

3   Make these sentences less repetitive by using pronouns.

(a) Lisa took Lisa's dog for a walk in the park because Lisa's dog had been indoors all day.

(b) Mark walked into the classroom, Mark found an empty seat and he sat down on the seat.

(c) Sian's mother told Sian to go to the shops to buy milk because Sian's mother had run out of milk.

4   Identify which part of speech the words in bold belong to in the following sentences.

(a) I **set** the table with our new **set** of cutlery.

(b) Can somebody sitting **close** to the door please **close** it?

(c) It would only be **fair** if everybody rode the merry-go-round at the **fair**.

(d) My good mood will **last** until the end of the day as long as I don't come **last** in the race.

Test
Test time: 10:00

It was the first day of school and I was excited. I skipped merrily along the pavement, through the park and into the playground. "Wow!" I thought to myself as I saw the crowds of boys and girls chatting and laughing loudly. It had been a long holiday but now I was ready to get back to lessons, football practice and seeing my friends. I spotted Jim sprinting towards me. He jumped over a bench, clipped his heel and tumbled helplessly onto the gravel. "Ouch!" he exclaimed but then a deep laugh erupted from his mouth and we both started to giggle. Jim was my best friend. We had known each other forever because our mums are best friends too. We looked out for each other at school although he had spent the whole summer in Spain so I hadn't seen him for months. "Hey!" I said as I helped him up from the ground.

5   Find and list three verbs from the passage above.   (3)

6   Find and list three adverbs from the passage above.   (3)

7   Which part of speech does the word 'myself' belong to?   (1)

8   Which part of speech does the word 'he' belong to?   (1)

9   Which part of speech does the word 'Spain' belong to?   (1)

10 Find and list three prepositions from the passage above.   (3)

Test 1: Spelling, punctuation and grammar

You should aim to complete this test in one hour.

Read the following passage and underline the correctly spelled word from each group.

1   As Simon **grabed/grabbed/grabbt** his bag and ran out of the **bilding/bulding/building** he could still hear his teacher's words **echoing/echowing/echoeing** in his head. He could not **discribe/describe/describ** how **embarassed/embarrassed/embarrased** he was at being told off in front of all of his **frends/friends/freinds**. He shook his head in **dissbelief/disbelief/disbeleif**. He hadn't even done anything *that* **unplesant/unpleasant/unplaesant** this time! It had just **occurred/ocurred/occured** to him, halfway through the morning, that this **paticular/particuler/particular** science lesson was a bit boring. It needed someone to make it a bit more **exiting/exciting/exsiting**. Mr Jones was being **extreemly/extremely/extremly** **unnreasonable/unreasonable/unresonable** about it all. It was just a few chemicals. He hadn't intended to blow a hole in the wall so that everyone could see **strait/straigt/straight** through it into the **library/libray/librarey**. He had put on his most **soleum/solem/solemn** face and **apoligised/apologised/appologised** but Mr Jones had **immediately/imediately/immediatly** taken the **necessary/necesary/neccesary** precautions, removed him from the classroom and sent him **diretly/directly/directley** to the Headmaster's office. Mr Watkins had decided to **ennsure/ensure/enssure** that this type of unruly **behavior/behaviour/behavier** never happened again. He had marched Simon back into the classroom and told him off for a full five **minuets/minits/minutes** in front of the whole class. He had then excluded him from school for a week. Simon felt the **familiar/familier/familliar** feeling of dread as he trudged home **slowley/slowely/slowly**.   (25)

2   A girl, **who's/whose** name was Francesca, was walking to school with her mother. As she **past/passed** the shop she asked her mother if she could **by/buy** her **some/sum** sweets. Francesca's mother said that **there/their/they're** was **no/know** need **four/for** sweets as she had just eaten a huge bowl of **cereal/serial** covered in sugar **four/for** breakfast so she wasn't **allowed/aloud** sweets. Unfortunately, Francesca did not **here/hear** her mother as she was **to/two/too** excited by the **sight/site** of a grizzly **bare/bear** that was galloping down the **road/rode**. She tugged at her mother's arm, squealing 'Over **there/their/they're** Mummy!' She didn't think her mother **wood/would** listen to her, so she **through/threw** her arms around her mother's knees and the **pear/pair** of them toppled **to/two/too** the ground.   (20)

The punctuation and capital letters in these sentences are not always correct. However, not all of the sentences contain mistakes. Note down the letter of the section with the mistake in it where there is one, and if you think there are no mistakes, write N for 'None'.

3   On wednesday I am going to the cinema with Rory, Adam and Sam.
       A   B   C   D   E   N

4   The children from Millbank school are going on a trip to France next April.
       A   B   C   D   E   N

5   Mary Ford, whose birthday is next Friday is my best friend.
       A   B   C   D   E   N

6   "Please put out the rubbish Paul," said his mother, as she took another chocolate.
       A   B   C   D   E   N

7   We are going to London to see Buckingham Palace the Science Museum and Tower Bridge.
       A   B   C   D   E   N

8   We are going to stay with my grandparents, who live in Manchester, for Christmas.
       A   B   C   D   E   N

9   My brother and i love to watch nature programmes such as *Springwatch* and *The Blue Planet*.
       A   B   C   D   E   N

10 We must do the shopping, clean the car, mow the lawn and bake a cake
       A   B   C   D   E   N

11 John has many pets, including four cats, two dogs, twelve goldfish, and an ancient parrot.
          A   B   C   D   E   N

12 When we go on holiday to Turkey, we will fly out from Gatwick Airport.
       A   B   C   D   E   N   (10)

Write out these sentences, adding capital letters, full stops, commas, speech marks, question marks, exclamation marks and apostrophes where necessary.

13 (a) where is your homework asked mrs danes the maths teacher   (2)

   (b) i think ive left it at home replied luke   (2)

   (c) that shouted mrs danes is the excuse you used last week and quite frankly i dont believe it   (2)

   (d) looking severely at luke mrs danes said see me at playtime and dont be late   (2)

   (e) yes miss replied luke   (2)

   (f) then under his breath he muttered you miserable old trout   (2)

The following paragraph is missing its punctuation. Rewrite it, adding in all of the missing punctuation.

14 my cat nigel theres a story behind the name but ill tell you that another time lived until the age of eighteen he was a remarkable cat he went blind at the age of two but somehow managed to cope with life very well indeed by using his other senses
    he could find his food by smelling for it and because he remembered that the cat-flap was just to the left of his food bowl he could easily find his way to the garden once there he felt his way to the lawn and would then run really fast to the end once or twice he forgot where the end was and crashed into the flowerbed but luckily he was not hurt   (18)

For each question, find and write down the words in the sentence that are stated in brackets at the end. For example: Everyone looked at the <u>boy</u> standing at the front of the <u>class</u>. (2 nouns)

15 "Mum, where's my bag?" shouted David.   (3 nouns) (3)

16 Everyone going on the school trip must bring a packed lunch.   (2 verbs) (2)

17 He ran quickly across the crowded classroom and nearly tripped over a huge bag.
(2 adjectives) (2)

18 Things were going badly for Simon. He had carelessly left his homework in his dad's car.
(2 adverbs) (2)

19 Megan told her a joke but she didn't laugh.   (2 pronouns) (2)

20 I thought the film started at seven, but when I got to the cinema I found it didn't begin
until eight.   (1 conjunction) (1)

21 I waited outside the supermarket next to the trolleys where Mum would meet me after
she had done the shopping.   (2 prepositions) (2)

For each question, write down the words that are asked for.

22 Choose two pronouns to fill the gaps in this sentence:

The work was so hard that _____ had to ask his teacher to help _____. (2)

23 Identify the word that shows what Alan <u>did</u> in this sentence:

Alan ran quickly so that he would be on time. (1)

24 Choose a conjunction to complete this sentence:

I like tennis _____ he prefers football. (1)

25 Identify the subordinate clause in this sentence:

Even though he had done little practice, Lloyd played very well. (1)

26 Identify the interjection in this sentence:

Ugh! That tastes disgusting! (1)

Rewrite the following passage, correcting the spelling, punctuation and grammar mistakes.

27 Last weak I visited my new senior school. I will be starting school their in september. The bilding is brand knew and the sports hall is quiet moden to. There was lots of amazing facilitys and I will be leaning lots of diffrent subjects at my new school, including spanish food tecnology Japanese and economics. many off my freinds from junior school are going to the same school as me in the autum and were all feeling very exited about it. Before my visit last week I has lots of questions that I wanted to find out the ansers to. How many pupils would there be in my class. would the teachers all be woman like they are at my junior school. Would I have ours of homework evry night. Luckily I had the chance to ask all these questions when I was being shown round by won of the currant Year 7 pupils. He was really friendly and helpfull and he didnt make me feel stupid for asking. He said that he was very nervos before he became a pupil they're but once he had been at the school four a few days he felt like hed allways been there he said that the teachers wasn't to strict and that there wasnt even much homework for the first half term. Now that I now a bit more about what to expect I'm really looking forwad to starting my new school. In fact I think its going to be amazing. (50)

Record your score and time here and at the start of the book.

Score [ ] / 155   Time [ ] : [ ]

Reading

Introduction

Different types of texts are written and structured in different ways. In an English exam you will be expected to read and understand (comprehend) different types of texts and you will also be expected to be able to write different types of texts in the writing section of the paper, (sometimes referred to as composition).

In order to make this easier for yourself, one thing you can do is learn to recognise the key features of these different text types. If you can identify which features belong to which type of text you will find it much easier to understand the texts you come across in exams. You will also find it much easier to write each type of text as you will have a checklist in your head of which features you should be including. This places you on step three of the Learning Ladder.

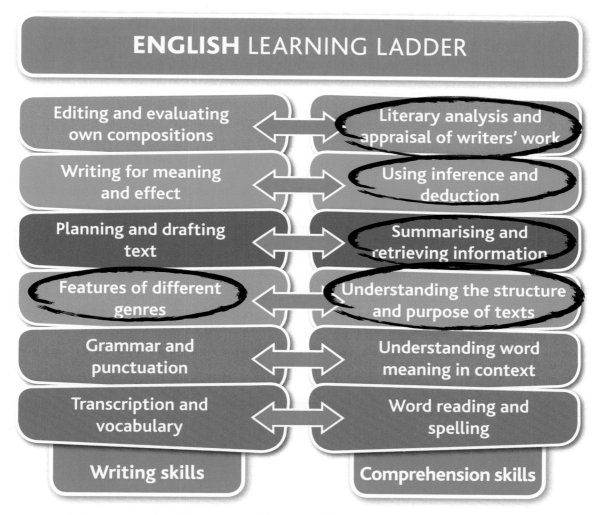

The purpose of the comprehension part of the exam is to test your ability to understand what you have read and you will be asked questions to test your understanding of different aspects of the text. There is a range of question types that you will encounter and you will need to use a number of strategies and skills to answer them.

In most comprehension exercises, the questions follow the text through in a logical order. This means that the first question is usually about the beginning of the text or poem and the last questions are often about the text as a whole. The questions tend to get more difficult as the test progresses and are therefore worth more marks. It is *incredibly important* to look at the number of marks available for each question as it guides you as to how long to spend on the question and how much detail is required in your written answer. Look for clues in the wording of the question as to how many points, reasons or examples are expected.

The skills relating to **closer analysis of texts** can be found on the **right-hand side** of the learning ladder, so you will climb steps four, five and six of the ladder by the end of the chapter. However, it is also important to glance at the left-hand side of the ladder as you can see how these skills relate to your own writing, which you will look at more closely in Chapter 3.

Advice for parents

Lots of children find comprehension the most difficult of all the skills to master in English. They often feel more confident about the writing section of the paper, but the 'unknown' element of the comprehension paper can be extremely daunting. With this in mind, this chapter aims to teach comprehension in an understandable and accessible way, reflecting and supporting a wide range of strategies being taught by English teachers within the classroom.

While practising strategies and completing practice papers are very important, one of the best ways to support your child's comprehension skills is to read aloud with them regularly and discuss the material they are reading. Be rigorous with your questions, asking your child to support their answers by pointing to or referencing something from the book. Encourage your child to read a wide range of text types including newspapers, plays, poetry and non-fiction. It is also very important for your child to see you reading different types of text in everyday life as it sends a strong message about the importance of reading.

When it comes to answering questions about texts, reading together is an excellent way to practise this skill. Try to ask analytical questions and encourage your child to read between the lines, make predictions and discuss the author's choices and techniques.

Remember, any discussions that you have with your child about texts of any type are supporting the work they will be doing at school and reinforcing and consolidating what they are being taught. At home these chats will be informal and, for some children, far less intimidating than being in a classroom situation. No matter how insignificant they seem to you, they can be hugely beneficial to your child.

- Read a range of material – fiction, non-fiction, short stories, poems, newspapers, blogs, etc. Get out of your comfort zone with your reading choices. The more genres you are familiar with, the easier your comprehension test will be.
- Make up your own comprehension questions for an extract or chapter of a book you are reading.
- Read a book that has been made into a film. You can then watch the film and discuss the similarities and differences.
- Listen to stories on an MP3 player or podcast and discuss them. This is good for long car journeys.
- Read two books by the same author and compare them.
- Read with your younger brothers and sisters and ask them questions about the text.
- Choose a picture to talk about and make up stories about what is happening in the picture. Magazines and newspapers are good places to find images.

Identifying text types

Skill definition: Understanding texts by identifying themes and conventions in a range of fiction and non-fiction writing.

Before tackling comprehension questions, it is important to have a sense of the type of text you are reading. This will help you to understand and answer the questions better. Each text type has its own particular conventions and features. Some overlap between genres and others are unique to one genre. Identifying which text type you are reading is the first step in successful understanding.

Fiction

Comprehension tasks often include narrative writing and you may also be asked to continue writing a story as part of the exam. Alternatively, you may be given a title and be asked to write a story to fit the title in the writing paper.

It is important to understand how to structure a short story, although the style and language will differ depending on the genre of story that you are writing (such as adventure, historical text, science fiction). You will have studied and written across a range of genres at school and you should be aware of which are your strongest, so these are the ones you should aim to use in an exam if the question gives you the opportunity to do so.

Classic narrative

This is a short story about a young boy, lost on the Underground.

Tom was excited. His father was finally taking him to the Natural History Museum to see the dinosaurs. He had been promising to bring him for months and now here they finally were, on the busy platform at the tube station, waiting for the train.

"Not long now, son," his father commented, but Tom's attention was elsewhere. On the
5 wall there was a poster advertising the latest *Lost Kingdom* film, his favourite series about an adventurous archaeologist, Dr Jack Rackler. He was so engrossed in the poster that he didn't see the train arrive. He didn't hear his father call him. He didn't see him step into the carriage. In fact, he only realised where he was as the train pulled away. His last glimpse of his father was his face whizzing past behind the glass doors, waving frantically. He was
10 suddenly all alone on the platform with no idea what to do next.

The platform was deserted but as he looked around he saw the silhouette of a stetson hat. It couldn't be … Could it? Standing at the end of the platform, clear as day, was Jack Rackler.

"What are you doing here on your own, young man?" he questioned. Tom was stunned,
15 silenced by disbelief.

"I … I … I lost my dad. We're supposed to be seeing the dinosaurs," he stuttered, looking around for any other people.

"Well then, we'd better get you to the Natural History Museum. It just so happens I'm going there myself."
20 As a train pulled up, Jack ushered Tom on and they sat together discussing archaeology, dinosaurs, movies, foreign lands and ancient creatures. Tom felt as if he was in a dream that he never wanted to end.

"Here's our stop," remarked Jack and off they stepped, climbed the stairs and found themselves outside the museum. Standing at the top of the steps looking panicked was
25 Tom's father. He approached him.

Full sentence

Problem

Clear beginning *Main characters*

Direct speech

"Dad, look, you'll never guess how I got here," Tom exclaimed. But as he turned around to introduce Jack to his dad, there was nobody there. He had vanished.

"Thank goodness you're OK!" his dad said. "I was so worried. Who did you say brought you here?"

30 "Ermmm … well … It was …" muttered Tom.

"Well you're safe and that's what matters," interrupted his dad. And off they went into the museum to see the dinosaurs. *Clear ending and solution*

Key features checklist

- Has a clear beginning, middle and end
- Usually includes between one and four main characters
- Features a conflict or problem and a solution
- Written in full sentences
- Often includes direct speech
- Includes action and description
- Divided into paragraphs

In addition to classic narrative, there are several other genres in fiction, each containing a set of characteristics that are listed below. Each list is followed by some examples of books which you could read to further prepare yourself.

Historical fiction

- Set in the past
- Often set during a particular historical event or period; for example, the First World War
- Details and description give more information about that period of time
- The plot links to the features of that historical period

Examples: *War Horse, Carrie's War, Goodnight Mister Tom, The Machine Gunners, Oliver Twist, The Eagle of the Ninth, Private Peaceful*

Adventure fiction

- Starts with a hook
- May include a journey or voyage
- Often takes place in an unknown or exotic location
- Clear series of interlinked dilemmas and problems
- Lots of action and dialogue
- Use of tension and cliffhangers
- Plot unfolds quickly
- Theme may be good overcoming evil or main characters overcoming adversity

Examples: *Treasure Island, Moby Dick, Wolf Brother, Journey to the River Sea, Swallows and Amazons, The Letter for the King*

Horror or ghost story

- Often set in the past
- Setting may be a haunted building or place
- Characters will see or be visited by ghosts or spirits

- There is often a mystery to solve, explaining why the ghost is present
- Tension and timing are key to building a frightening atmosphere
- It may seem that the characters are imagining the ghosts at first
- Information is slowly revealed to the reader

Examples: *Uncle Montague's Tales of Terror, The Graveyard Book, The Last of the Spirits, A Christmas Carol, Half a Creature from the Sea*

Fantasy fiction

- Invented settings and characters
- Often involves quests or long journeys of discovery
- Often includes magic powers and magical characters

Examples: *The Lord of the Rings, The Hobbit, Skellig, Harry Potter* series, *Narnia* series

Mystery

- A problem needs solving by a detective-type character
- A theft or murder may be the main event
- Each character has a link to the crime but only one is the criminal
- Tension is used and plot twists included to confuse the reader
- Clues are revealed including red herrings
- In the end the mystery is swiftly and clearly solved with one or more culprits
- Sometimes the detective has to use some specialist knowledge to solve the mystery, for example forensic knowledge

Examples: *The London Eye Mystery, Hacker, Stormbreaker* series, *His Dark Materials* trilogy, *The Laura Marlin Mysteries* series, *Millions*

Science fiction

- Set in the future, on this planet or in another world
- Based on some scientific understanding or development
- May have a mixture of reality and fantasy
- May cover the theme of good versus evil
- Scientific understanding often resolves the problem of the story
- May include real or invented scientific language or concepts

Examples: *The Hitchhiker's Guide to the Galaxy, A Wrinkle in Time, Phoenix, Cosmic, Larklight*

Myths and legends

- Traditional tales used to explain natural phenomena or to send a moral message
- Natural elements (wind, fire, etc.), gods, animals and supernatural forces may be involved
- Monsters or other fantastical characters may be used; for example, the Minotaur
- Simple start and clear problem or dilemma
- Clear resolution
- Often short in length
- A final line or comment summarises the story
- Legends in particular include historical characters or events; for example, King Arthur

Examples: *Percy Jackson* series, *Heroes of Olympus, Odd and the Frost Giants*

1 Imagine you have been asked to write a story with the title 'The Longest Night'. Think of three different ways to interpret the title, which would result in stories of different genres. For example, science fiction: a story about the Sun being stolen by an alien race or historical fiction: a story set during the Blitz in the Second World War. Write a short paragraph to explain each idea.

Poem

Some comprehension tests will ask you to read and respond to a poem. This can be a harder task than responding to a standard text as the language used in poetry has lots of meaning packed in. The questions may focus not just on the meaning of the poem but also the structure, punctuation, rhyme and rhythm and the poet's skill with language. Although poetry comprehensions do not come up very often, you should be prepared to tackle them just in case!

> This is a poem by a very famous American poet called Henry Wadsworth Longfellow who wrote poetry in the nineteenth century. In this poem, the writer expresses his feelings about the rain.

How beautiful is the rain!
After the dust and heat,
In the broad and fiery street, ——— Stanza
In the narrow lane,
5   How beautiful is the rain!

How it clatters along the roofs,
Like the tramp of hoofs——— Simile
How it gushes and struggles out ———→ Rhyme
From the throat of the overflowing spout!

10   Across the window-pane
It pours and pours; —— Repetition
And swift and wide,
With a muddy tide,   —— Onomatopoeia
Like a river down the gutter roars
15   The rain, the welcome rain!

From *Rain in Summer* by Henry Wadsworth Longfellow

Key features checklist

● Written in **stanzas** (verses)
● Creates word pictures using techniques including **similes**, **alliteration**, **onomatopoeia** and repetition
● Often has a distinctive rhythm
● Can (but does not have to) rhyme
● Not always written in full sentences

- Doesn't have to follow standard punctuation rules
- Can tell a story, describe something or express a feeling
- Does not have to use Standard English

2   Choose a poetry book from the library and read a selection of poems. Choose three of your favourites and identify the features described above.

Play script

As with poems, play scripts do not appear in comprehension tests as often as stories, but it is still important to understand the layout and features as you may be asked to continue the story in the form of a play script.

This scene is from a play in which a young girl named Anna is chosen to go on an expedition into space. A new planet has been discovered and she will be travelling along with scientists and politicians in order to make contact with the alien inhabitants.

Scene 1 ——————————— *Divided into scenes*   —— Long stage directions

Anna runs in from school. She has some very exciting news to tell her parents. Her mum is in the kitchen making the dinner. She turns round when she hears the door slam.
Anna: Mum! Mum!————————— Character's name ——— Punctuation
Mum: (surprised) What is it? Is everything alright?
5   Anna: (excitedly) I've got some amazing news!   Short stage direction
Anna moves closer to her mum and waves a piece of paper in front of her.
Mum: What exciting news?

Key features checklist

- Divided into scenes
- Names on the left followed by colons (:)
- Long stage directions in italics (and/or brackets) and in the present tense
- Short stage directions in brackets before the words that are spoken
- No speech marks
- Punctuation as normal
- Tells a story through stage directions and dialogue

3   Change the play script above into narrative text (in the style of a regular story). Think about how you will use speech punctuation.

4   Choose a short section from the book you are currently reading or another favourite story and transform the prose into a play script, remembering to include all the key features listed above. It is best to choose a passage that has some speech in it.

Non-fiction

Diary

Many people throughout history have written diaries; you may have read *The Diary of Anne Frank*, for example. The language used in diaries will vary depending on the age of the writer and the time at which it was written. Always put yourself in the author's shoes and consider how they feel and think.

This extract is taken from the diary of a ten-year-old girl called Lucy. Something very exciting has just happened to her so she has decided to write about it in her diary.

Dated entry ——————— 3 August 1997

Dear Diary, *Past tense*

Today was the best day of my life! I can't believe that something so amazing actually happened to me! When I woke up this morning I had no idea that something so incredible would happen. I'd just finished eating my breakfast and Liam was being annoying as

5   always, when it happened. *Feeling/emotion*

I had woken up expecting just another boring day because even though it's the summer holidays Mum and Dad are at work so every day's pretty much the same. Me and Liam get up, have breakfast and get along OK for about half an hour and then he annoys me so much that I have to get away from him! Well, this morning was no different. I stormed

10   upstairs because if I had to look at him for two more seconds I was going to explode but when I opened my bedroom door there was nothing there. Literally nothing. I'll write more later. I can hear Mum coming upstairs … *Informal language*

Key features checklist

- Dated entries
- Written in the past tense
- Informal language
- May be written in non-Standard English, depending on where the writer comes from
- Explains what has happened (facts/information)
- Includes feelings and emotions
- Written in chronological order

Train   •

5   Write the diary entry, no longer than half a side of A4, for the most memorable day of your life.

Explanation

Sometimes in an exam you may be given an explanation text to read. This will be similar to a set of instructions or a non-chronological report and will usually be a partly visual text. It is likely to include pictures or diagrams, boxed text, subheadings and lists and it is important to pay careful attention to these stylistic features. These are often overlooked by pupils in exams as they only look for the answers in the main body of the text when they should be looking elsewhere.

This explanation, 'How to build a fire', is taken from a book about traditional skills that are being lost in today's modern world. This section explains how to build and light a fire indoors.

Introduction

Throughout history, people have used fires to provide warmth and light. In modern households in the twentieth century, most people have the luxury of central heating to keep their houses warm, but in recent years, wood
5 burning stoves have regained popularity in the UK and may now be found in the lounges and living rooms of many households across the country.

To light a fire in a stove or wood-burner there are several techniques, but a popular and reliable method
10 begins with a stack of kindling*. Place two pieces of kindling parallel to one another so that another two pieces can be placed at ninety-degree angles on the outside edges to form a square. Repeat this process several times until a small 'log-cabin-like' structure is
15 formed, with lots of gaps for air to pass through. Drop small balls of scrunched up newspaper into the centre of the kindling structure. Place a log on top of this (bark side down). Use a long match to light the newspaper at the base; the kindling should catch fire easily, heating
20 the underside of the log and the entire structure should collapse down into a hot, burning pile, with the log resting on top, already alight.

■ Ensure that the vents on the wood-burner are fully open before lighting the stove

Note: The kindling will take about five minutes to begin to burn briskly and the logs 10–15 minutes to catch fire. The stove will take around 30 minutes to be burning well.

Paragraph with topic sentence   Plain, simple language   Imperative verb

* kindling – dry wood or sticks used to light a fire

Key features checklist

- Introduction sets the scene/gives information about the topic
- Written in paragraphs starting with a topic sentence
- Does not give a biased view
- Chronological order
- Includes pictures, diagrams and charts
- Third person narrator
- Formal language and style
- Present tense
- Imperative (bossy) verbs
- Plain, simple language

Train

6   Think of an activity that you know how to do or skill that you have. It may be building a particular model from Lego®, baking a cake, playing a scale on the piano, designing a website, etc. Go and make or do the thing you have decided on and write bullet points as you go along that you would include in an explanation text.

Persuasive

Persuasive texts, as their name suggests, are intended to persuade others to see things from a particular point of view. They are often used in advertising and often use very strong language to make a point.

This text is an extract from a speech given by United States President, Barack Obama. He made the speech to the American people when he began his second term of office in January 2013.

Gets the reader/listener on your side   *First person narrator*

My fellow Americans, the oath I have sworn before you today, like the one recited by others who serve in this Capitol, was an oath to God and country, not party or faction. And we must faithfully execute that pledge during the duration of our service. But the words I spoke today are not so different from the oath that is taken each
5   time a soldier signs up for duty or an immigrant realizes her dream. My oath is not so different from the pledge we all make to the flag that waves above and that fills our hearts with pride.

Ideas repeated in threes

They are the words of citizens and they represent our greatest hope. You and I, as citizens, have the power to set this country's course. You and I, as citizens, have the
10   obligation to shape the debates of our time -- not only with the votes we cast, but with the voices we lift in defence of our most ancient values and enduring ideals.   *Emotive language*

Let us, each of us, now embrace with solemn duty and awesome joy what is our lasting birthright. With common effort and common purpose, with passion and dedication, let us answer the call of history and carry into an uncertain future that
15   precious light of freedom.   *Repetition of phrases for emphasis*

Key features checklist

- Strong, emotive language
- Ideas repeated in threes so that the audience will remember them
- First person narrator
- Rhetorical questions – do not require an answer but used to make a point
- Opening statement introduces point of view
- Good reasons and evidence
- Gets the reader/listener interested and on the writer's/speaker's side
- Short sentences for emphasis
- Makes the reader/listener think that the writer's/speaker's viewpoint is the only correct one
- Clearly biased – only one viewpoint is offered

Train

7   Imagine you need to persuade your parents to do something. It may be to book a holiday, buy you a particular gift, etc. Make a spider diagram of persuasive phrases and ideas that you could use to get what you want.

Discursive

You may be given a discursive text to read in an exam as they are generally quite complex, involving lots of arguments for and against a topic. The language is formal and sophisticated, therefore they are challenging texts to read. Another name for this type of writing is a balanced argument, as it addresses both points of view on a theme.

This piece is taken from a school magazine written by pupils in Year 10. The article is about the controversial issue of fox-hunting and it includes a range of points both for and against banning the sport.

— Starts with a question   — Introduction explains the topic

Should fox-hunting be banned?

Fox-hunting is the name given to the tradition of chasing wild foxes with a pack of hounds. It has been used as a way of controlling foxes ever since we started farming animals to sell. According to surveys, 60 per cent of people think it is a cruel sport that
5 should be banned; however the other 40 per cent believe that this ancient tradition should continue.

— Argument against ban   — Statistics

One argument made by those in favour of fox-hunting is that foxes are pests that need to be controlled. If a fox kills a farmer's animals then the farmer has no animals to sell. This means that the farmer will lose money and will find it harder to make a living by selling
10 his livestock. This will then have an effect of his family and his standard of living. A second argument for fox-hunting is that it is a tradition that dates back to 1534 and is therefore a significant part of our country's history and heritage.

— Argument for ban   — Fact

However, many people would argue that foxes are not dangerous predators and that they do not kill a large enough number of farm animals for them to be hunted and killed
15 by dogs. Furthermore, the trauma experienced by the fox during the hunt is considered by many people to be barbaric and unnecessary.

— Connective

In conclusion, although there are many arguments for and against this issue, I personally think that fox-hunting should be banned. Although there are many reasons given by farmers and traditionalists, I think that fox-hunting is horrific. The fox is a living creature
20 and it should be treated with the same respect afforded to other animals.

— Conclusion

Key features checklist

- Starts with a question
- Introduction explains the topic
- Main paragraphs give arguments for and against
- Facts, figures and statistics
- Impersonal style and formal language
- Connectives
- Conclusion summarises main points and gives personal opinion

Train

8   Think of an important issue, either from the news or from your school life, for example: Should recycling be made compulsory by law? Should children wear uniform? Make a list of points for and against in order to address the question.

Autobiography, biography and recount

Texts that tell somebody's life story (usually somebody famous or important) are called autobiographies and biographies. Both of these text types are very common in comprehension exams. These texts are usually written by adults so the language is sophisticated and they feature lots of personal details which can be analysed closely. The difference between the two types is that an autobiography is written by the person who is the subject of the book. A biography is written about somebody by another writer. They share many common features.

First person narrator   *Date*

This extract is taken from the autobiography of a Science teacher and amateur archaeologist. This chapter covers the writer's childhood and early life.

    I was born on May 13th 1978 in a place called Chatham, Kent. The first house I remember living in was on Honeysuckle Close and the thing I remember most clearly about it was the garden. It was the size of a jungle and was perfect for adventuring. From the age of five I used to head off down the garden, dragging my long-suffering mother

5   with me, into the dense maze of trees and bushes and pretend that I was off to discover dinosaurs. My parents tell me that I was obsessed with dinosaurs, from the first moment that I could turn the pages of a book. I suppose that's how I've come to do the job I do now, but I will get to that later …   *Emotive language*   *Key event from the narrator's life*

    I had a very happy childhood. I lived at Honeysuckle Close for seven years. When

10 I was four, my brother Ben came along and then shortly afterwards my mother had a baby girl, so there were three of us in total. The age gap between me and my brother and sister was only four or five years, but it felt huge when we were young. I made the most of being the eldest, though, by bossing them around and laying down the rules for all of our games.   *Past tense*   *People who influenced the narrator*

15 My parents were both originally from Poland, but, along with their families, they had moved to the UK back in the 1960s, so they had been living in the country for a long time when I was born. That didn't mean that they had forgotten their Polish roots, though. In our household my parents held on to many customs and traditions from their past, so my childhood was an interesting mixture of Polish and British culture.

Key features checklist

- First person narrator (autobiography) or third person narrator (biography)
- Includes key events from the narrator's life
- Chronological order
- Refers to people who influenced the narrator
- Includes dates and details
- Written in the past tense
- Uses time connectives
- Includes emotive language

A recount text tells the story of (or 'recounts') something that has happened and is often a specific event. So a biography is also a recount, just about an individual's life. Newspaper and magazine articles can also be recounts, often using less emotive language to explain something either current or historical.

Train
•••••••••••••••••••••••••••••••

9   Use the following list to make notes in preparation for a short biographical piece about a person you are interested in learning more about. You may need to do some research on the internet or in a library: birth year and place, family (including siblings), school life and education, significant achievements, influences.

Newspaper/magazine article

Newspaper and magazine articles often feature in comprehension tasks. They are written using a formal style and are complex texts, requiring a good understanding of style, language and layout. It is important to remember that, as with all non-fiction texts, the layout and style are just as important as the content, so you must think carefully about *how* the text is written and laid out, not just what it is about.

This article is taken from a local newspaper. The article is about a dog that performed a daring rescue.

Byline

BOY SAVED FROM DROWNING BY DOG ——— *Bold, catchy headline*

By John Carpenter *Brief overview*   *Fact*

On Wednesday morning an extraordinary event happened in a park in Manchester. Louis Fletcher was walking his dog, Rex, a golden retriever, around Green Street Park when Rex ran off into the trees, towards the lake. It was 8.30 am and there were very few people around at the time. *Past tense*

5   Louis, 15, from Crouch Lane said, "I was surprised by Rex tearing off like that. He is normally very well-behaved. I followed him as I didn't want him to get lost."

When Louis caught up with Rex, the dog had already dived into the lake and was swimming out towards the island in the centre.

"As I approached I realised that there was someone in the water," said Louis.

10   It appeared that Rex had leapt in to save a young boy who was in trouble in the water.

Quick-thinking Louis, who has been a cub scout from a very young age, immediately called the emergency services, who were on the scene within minutes.

Firefighters quickly rescued the six-year-old boy, who cannot be named at this time, from the lake. *Opinion*

15   Brian Young, a firefighter who arrived on the scene, said of the event, "Louis' quick thinking and sensible actions certainly saved this young boy's life."

The young boy in question was taken to a nearby hospital for a check-up, but has since made a full recovery. The police are not treating the incident as suspicious.

Key features checklist

- Written in columns
- Bold, catchy headline
- Brief byline
- Brief overview paragraph giving outline of content
- Past tense
- Answers the questions who, what, where, when, why, how
- Can use formal or more informal language (depending on the publication)
- Includes fact and opinion

Train ●

10 Ask your parents to choose and cut out a suitable newspaper article for you to read. Highlight or make a note of all the key features from the list above that you can spot.

Using strategies for tackling comprehension questions

Skill definition: Developing strategies for tackling comprehension questions.

In any comprehension task there are certain strategies that you can use to help you. You need to learn these strategies and practise using them regularly so that in an exam you use them without even having to think about it.

The text

When you are reading the text in a comprehension test, it is important that you read the words carefully and really think about what you are reading. If you haven't understood what the text is about you will find it hard to answer questions about it and this will cost you time later on. At the start of the paper you will usually be given guidance on how much time to spend reading, for example, 'You have 10 minutes' reading time'. You *must* read the text at least twice, and ideally you should try to read it three times, but you should also aim to stick to the time guidelines given.

Your first reading should give you an overview of what the text is about. Try to picture what is happening in your mind so that you have a clear idea of what is going on. You should then read it again. Lots of children find it helpful to make notes next to each paragraph or stanza to summarise what each one is about or to highlight important words and phrases. When you are reading you need to remember that it is not a race! Although you will be keen to start writing your answers, you will gain more marks if you read the text carefully.

You will often find numbers written at the side of the text. These are the line numbers and will usually be in multiples of 5. They are there to help you find the lines easily and to help you refer to sections of text in your answers.

The questions

After you have read the text you should read the questions carefully. The questions will usually get harder as you go along. You must make sure that each answer is focused and actually answers the question asked. You should usually answer in full sentences unless the question asks you to do otherwise.

To help you focus your answers and include the relevant information it can be helpful to highlight key words in the questions. For example, in the question: 'What shape is Miss Johnson's face?' the key word is 'shape', so your answer must include a shape. Your answer might be: 'Miss Johnson's face is oval-shaped.'

If you are struggling to work out what the key words are, imagine you are texting the question to a friend and think about which parts you would include. If the question is: 'In line 5, what simile is used to describe the tree?' the key words are 'line 5, simile, tree'.

The marks

Next to each question there should be a number of marks written in brackets. It is very important to look at the number of marks available for a question as this will give you an idea of how much to write in your answer.

As a general rule, to gain 1 mark you need to make one point. Sometimes the question will make this very clear, by saying, 'Find two pieces of evidence that show that this story was set a long time ago.'

However, sometimes a question might say, 'What do we learn about Lisa's character in lines 4–5?' (2 marks). For 2 marks you will need to find two separate things that we learn about Lisa in those lines.

Sometimes you may be asked to 'give evidence' or 'quote' from the text. For instance:

'What kind of person is Mrs Smith? Give evidence from the passage to support your answer.' (4)

As you need to give evidence, 4 marks will be awarded for two ideas about Mrs Smith (2 marks) with a piece of evidence for each (2 more marks).

POINT   EVIDENCE
Mrs Smith has a bad temper. We know this because the passage says, 'Mrs Smith shouted at the postman.'

POINT   EVIDENCE
We know Mrs Smith is also a greedy person, because the passage says, 'She always took more than her fair share.'

> If you write a long answer for a 1-mark question, you may run out of time for the longer questions at the end, which are worth more marks. Keep your answers as short and precise as you can, while covering all the points required. You should never write the same answer for more than one question and don't repeat the same point many times in one answer as you won't get the marks more than once for the same point and you will waste time.

Multiple-choice questions

Sometimes in a comprehension test you may be given a selection of answers to choose from. If you come across this type of question it is still helpful to highlight the key words. With this type of question you may be able to spot the correct answer quickly and easily, but if you are finding it harder, a useful strategy is to go through each answer, crossing out those that are wrong until you are left with the right answer. Always choose an answer. Never leave multiple-choice questions blank. Multiple choice questions are generally worth one mark each.

Train •

1   Read the questions below and identify the words that tell you what to include in your answer.

   (a) How many children are waiting on the platform?

   (b) What colour is the rabbit that escapes from the hutch?

   (c) In line 7, which word shows Mr Philips is angry?

   (d) Find three things that prove that this passage is set in Victorian times.

   (e) Explain the meaning of the word 'tentative' in your own words.

   (f) How do we know that Mrs Moody is not a very clever person? Give evidence from the text to support your answer.

When you are writing your answer to the question, it is best to use your own words. You may be explicitly asked to do this in some questions. This shows that you have understood what the passage is about. However, sometimes in a comprehension test, you may be asked to 'give evidence' or 'quote' from the text. This means you need to copy out the exact words from the passage. If you are copying out from the passage you should show this by putting 'inverted commas' around the words you are copying out. This shows the person marking your work that these words are not your own.

Understanding the purpose, audience and structure of texts

Skill definition: Understanding *why* a text was written and *who* it was written for.

When you are asked about the purpose of a text, you need to consider a number of things: the text type, the audience and the structure of the text.

Purpose

In many comprehension tests (particularly on non-fiction texts) there will be a question about the purpose of the text. When answering these you need to think about why the text has been written. Use the following table as a starting point:

Text type	General purpose
Story	To provide entertainment; some stories, such as fables, teach a moral or ethical lesson
Poetry	To provide entertainment or evoke an emotional response
Explanation text	To give detailed information on a particular topic
Instruction text	To give detailed step-by-step guidance about how to do or make something
Speech	To inform or persuade, depending on the context
Letter	To share information, to complain or to persuade, depending on the context
Play script	To instruct actors how to perform a play, TV show or film

Audience

Most texts are written with a particular reader in mind. The type of language used will help you to work out who the audience of the text is.

Type of language	What it tells you
Formal or informal?	Formal language suggests that the audience is not someone familiar to the writer or that the writing has a serious purpose. Informal language suggests the reader is well-known to the writer or is a young child – the language has a more friendly and relaxed feel.
Simple or complex?	Simple language may be used for a younger audience or in an information text where transmitting information clearly is the purpose of the text. Complex language is often used in technical writing where the audience is already well-versed or expert in the topic (e.g. a scientific journal).
Literal or figurative?	Non-fiction texts largely use literal language but narrative and descriptive writing uses figurative language to help the reader build a vivid picture of an imagined story or place.

> This list does not contain every type of language and there are some exceptions. For example, in a persuasive speech, figurative language may be used to help the listener engage with the topic and understand the speaker's point of view more deeply.

Structure

The structure of a text refers to the order and layout of the information. When thinking about the purpose of a text, consider what it looks like and how it has been put together. Some features and their functions are listed on the next page.

Feature	Function
Paragraphs	To separate different topics or groups of information; in a story, they are used to separate different parts of the plot
Subheadings	To help a reader navigate a text and indicate what each section is going to be about; this is important in non-fiction in particular as a reader may not need to read the whole text in order
Text boxes	To draw attention to key information or summarised information
Bullet points	To highlight key points or facts
Captions	To give more detailed information or background about a picture or diagram
Contents/index	To help a reader navigate a text
Glossary	To give definitions of key words

In addition to these more obvious, physical structural features, in fiction, think about other features that may add to the structure:

- Cliffhanger – encourages the reader to read on and adds tension.
- Short sentences or paragraphs – slow the action down and draw attention to a particular event.
- Flashback– gives background to the main story.
- Repetition – emphasises a particular event or characteristic.

Train

1   Read the following short extract and decide what the **purpose** of the text is:

On the afternoon of Friday 2 January, Brian Smith, aged ten, witnessed an extraordinary event. It was unlike anything he had seen before. As he was cycling home from school, Brian, who lives on North Street, noticed a large gap in the hedge outside his neighbour's house. When he stopped his bicycle and looked through the hole he was astonished by what he saw.

Test

Test time: 05:00

2   How do you know the following text was written for young children?   (3)

John and Sarah liked to go to the park. The swings were their favourite place to play. Every Saturday they went to the playground. John went on the blue swing. Sarah went on the red swing. Sometimes they went on the green slide too.

3   How do you know this is an instructional text?   (3)

To cook a roast dinner successfully you need to:

1   Preheat the oven to Gas Mark 4.
2   Put the meat in a roasting tin in the oven.
3   Prepare the vegetables.
4   Lay the table.
5   Let the meat rest for 20 minutes after cooking.

4   What is the purpose of this text and how do you know?   (4)

Exercise is the most important way to keep healthy. Everyone knows that to look after our bodies, we need to move them regularly. When was the last time you really felt your heart beat fast? If you can't remember then perhaps you need to consider doing some more exercise: try swimming, running or walking. Choose an activity you enjoy and perhaps do it with some friends. Once you get into a habit you'll wonder how you ever got by without exercise before. You won't regret it!

Summarising key ideas

Skill definition: Summarising the main ideas drawn from more than one paragraph in fiction and non-fiction texts.

Summarising means picking out the key ideas or themes from a text. In many comprehension tests you will need to show that you can give an overview of a story, a character, a setting or a mood. You may need to show that you can give a short summary of what a particular paragraph or section is about. This often requires you to use your own words to describe something. You may also need to step back and consider the text as a whole.

Some examples of questions about summarising are listed below:

- What is your impression of the character of Sam in this story?
- How would you summarise the author's opinion in this speech?
- Explain what happened to the boat in your own words.

To answer these questions, there are some steps you can take:

1 Highlight relevant information in the passage.

2 Think of synonyms to help you explain something in your own words.

3 Identify the important information: if something is repeated in the text, you only need to mention it once in a summary.

4 Do not add or change any information when you summarise; this is an overview **not** a continuation of the story.

5 Be succinct: use as few words as you can without losing the meaning.

6 When you make an observation about a setting, character or opinion, make sure it is backed up in more than one place in the text. A summary should be an overview rather than a collection of individual comments. For example, a character who is almost always grumpy but smiles once in the text is generally a grumpy character and should be summarised as such.

7 Consider what a character or author says and does and put these actions together in one or two adjectives. For example, a character who skips into a room, smiles widely, greets everyone and engages in lively conversation may be summarised as cheerful and friendly.

8 If you are asked to summarise a particular element of a text, make sure you only address that. For example, if you are asked to summarise the arguments in favour of less homework, you should only refer to the arguments in favour, not against.

Train

1   Read the following extract and make notes to summarise what is happening in each paragraph.

This passage is taken from the novel *Lionboy* by Zizou Corder. This book is about a boy called Charlie Ashanti who is able to speak cat – the language of all wild and domestic cats. This unusual talent helps him on his quest to find his kidnapped parents who have discovered a cure for asthma. The book is set in the future.

It was mid-afternoon when the great crimson ship came through the electricity farm – ranks of ocean windmills, like an army of giant propellers on sticks – into the harbour at Le Havre. Charlie found that he was very glad to see land again, although he had hardly noticed missing it. As soon as they were docked he ran down the gangplank on to the

5   big concrete quay, desperate to find a cat with some news. As he landed his legs jarred horribly – how very solid the ground seemed, after his days at sea!

'Hey there, Lionboy!' called a voice from the deck behind him. It was Major Tib. 'Y'all better get right back on board now. We don't do shore leave without leave. Get back in here and help Maccomo. There's plenty work to be done.'

10   Turning back, disappointed, to the ship, Charlie saw a most peculiar sight. A great crane had been waiting for them on the quay when they cruised in, looking red and white against the sky. It had now sort of leaned in towards the ship, where the entire crew seemed to be scurrying about on deck at the foot of one of the masts. A huge chain hung from the crane, and was, Charlie realized, being attached near the base of the mast. Another chain hung

15 in mid-air – no, it was moving. Halfway up the mast another knot of sailors were busying themselves with something …

Suddenly a cry went up, the sailors all stood back and down as if in a single movement, and the mast was uprooted like a great tree in a high wind, or a giant weed in the hand of a giant gardener. Where it had stood tall and proud, it now lay flat in the air, hanging from

20 the chains, flying slowly and ponderously towards the quay.

'What's happening?' cried Charlie to one of the harbourguys standing by him on the quay.

'Stand back!' shouted the man, as the mast lurched through the air in their direction. 'Way back, stand back.'

2   Read the following recount from a school newsletter. Summarise what is happening in each paragraph.

Year 5 Trip to Sussex

Last Friday, Year 5 returned from their four-day cross-curricular residential trip to Sussex. They were accompanied on the trip by Mrs Jones, Mrs Miller, Ms Gurung, Mrs Lancaster and Miss Perez, who all agreed that the trip was a huge success!

Wednesday brought more fine weather and the girls spent an incredibly interesting morning
5 at the *Mary Rose* exhibition in Portsmouth, followed by a trip up the Spinnaker Tower. They had a great time leaping around on the glass floor, 100 metres up in the air! Mrs Jones, on the other hand, did not have such a great time due to her vertigo (fear of heights).

Thursday brought more hot weather and a day at the Weald and Downland Open-Air Museum where the girls donned their Tudor costumes, took part in apothecary and Tudor
10 farming workshops and indulged in a spot of maypole dancing. They then spent a fantastic afternoon at the beach building sandcastles before taking part in a talent show at the hotel.

On Friday the girls packed their suitcases, checked out of the hotel and travelled to Pagham Harbour Nature Reserve where they had great fun getting their hands dirty while pond-dipping, mud-sifting and hunting for minibeasts. By the end of the afternoon they
15 were all tired and looking forward to seeing their families again, but they all agreed that they had had a lovely time and hadn't missed their parents half as much as they expected to!

Test
● ● ● ● ● ● ● ● ● ● ● ● ● ● ● ● ● ●   Test time: 15:00

3   Reread the fiction extract above and answer the following question.

Summarise Charlie's opinion about the voyage he has just returned from. Refer to the text in your answer.   (2)

4   Reread the non-fiction extract above and answer the following question.

Summarise the overall success of the school trip. Refer to the text in your answer.   (2)

Using clues to find definitions

Skill definition: Establishing the meaning of unknown words using grammatical features and the context of the text.

Don't worry if you don't understand every single work in a text – you won't be the only one! Some words you can get away with just getting the gist of and still get the overall meaning of the text. In some tests you will be asked to give a definition or synonym (word with the same meaning) as one of the questions. This requires you to consider a number of things to help you if you don't already know what the words means:

● Can you use the rest of the sentence to work it out?

> Behind him where the walls were nearest could dimly be seen coats of mail, helms and axes, swords and spears hanging;
>
> From *The Hobbit* by J. R. R. Tolkien

Question 1   What is a 'helm'?   (1)

Here, the word is in a list of other weapons and so you can reasonably assume it is something similar.

● Can you use the part of speech to work out what it might mean?

> Mr McAlister was a short-tempered, difficult troublemaker who was always starting arguments. His cantankerous personality made him unpopular with the other residents.

Question 2   What does 'cantankerous' mean?   (1)

As the word is placed before a noun, it is likely to be an adjective. Now think about what we know about Mr McAlister. He is not a nice man so it is likely that cantankerous is something unpleasant. In the previous sentence he is described as argumentative. This is what cantankerous means.

● Is an explanation given elsewhere in the text?

> In many villages, the apothecary was a well-respected and trusted man. When people required treatments for illnesses and sicknesses, his potions and pills were often their first option as our modern chemists and pharmacies did not exist so long ago.

Question 3   What was an 'apothecary'?   (1)

From the first sentence, it is clear that it is some kind of person as it says 'man'. The passage goes on to talk about ill people, potions and pills, suggesting he provided some kind of treatment. It then refers to a lack of chemists, suggesting he was the old-fashioned alternative.

● Does it look or sound like any other words? Can you use your knowledge of spelling to help you?

He tried to read the map but it was smudged by the rain and was totally incomprehensible.

Question 4   What does "incomprehensible" mean?   (1)

If you look at the word, you can see 'in' at the beginning, which is a prefix meaning 'not'. In the middle you can see 'comprehen', which is close to 'comprehend'. This suggests it is something to do with not understanding. As the map was smudged, it is logical that it could not be understood.

> You are usually asked for the meaning of the word in a particular context so be careful with words that have more than one meaning. Always look back at the text and make sure you have found the correct meaning as it is used there.

Train

1   Give a definition for each of the words in bold in this passage.

> From Troy, winds cast Ulysses and his fleet upon the coast of the Cicons, a people hostile to the Grecians. Landing his forces, he laid **siege** to their chief city, Ismarus, which he took, and with it much spoil, and slew many people. But success proved fatal to him; for his soldiers, **elated** with the spoil, and the good store of provisions which they found in that
> 5   place, fell to eating and drinking, forgetful of their safety, till the Cicons, who inhabited the coast, had time to **assemble** their friends and allies from the interior; who, **mustering** in **prodigious** force, set upon the Grecians, while they **revelled** and feasted, and slew many of them, and recovered the spoil. They, dispirited and thinned in their numbers, with difficulty made their retreat good to the ships.
>
> From *The Adventures of Ulysses* by Charles Lamb

2   Underline or highlight the parts of these words that might help you to work out their meaning.

(a) disassemble
(b) predetermine
(c) contraindicate
(d) unaccustomed
(e) unchangeable

Test   Test time: 10:00

As we arrived at the aquarium, we were mesmerised by the plethora of colours and creatures on display. From simple orange goldfish to resplendent zebrafish and formidable piranhas, our eyes were assaulted by these florid sights. Of all of the tank-dwellers, my absolute favourite was the Siamese fighting fish. Its featherlike fins undulated in the water like fluttering eyelashes.

What is the meaning of the following words?

3   plethora   4   resplendent   5   formidable   6   florid   7   undulated

Retrieving specific information in fiction and non-fiction texts

Skill definition: Retrieving and presenting information from a fiction or non-fiction text to answer a specific question.

In most comprehension exercises, the simpler questions ask you to retrieve (find) specific information and they are often worth 1 or 2 marks. They usually focus on the place, time, people and events in the text and answering this type of question usually involves writing down a word or phrase from the passage. Here are some examples of information retrieval questions:

● Who was outside the window?
● What time of year was it when the accident happened?
● What was the boy doing in the playground?
● Which boy is the youngest in this extract?

Hopefully you have noticed that the important words in these types of question are 'who', 'what', 'where', 'when' and 'which'. If you can answer these questions, you are well on your way to understanding the whole text.

When you are answering information retrieval questions there is a simple pattern that you should follow. If the question asks:

● '**Who** is eating?', your answer should replace the word 'who' with the name of the character. For example, '**Ahmed** is eating.'
● '**When** did the car break down?', your answer should begin with the subject and end with the answer. For example, 'The car broke down **on Saturday morning**.'
● '**What** was Mum eating?' you should rearrange the question to make it into a statement. For example, 'Mum was eating **a banana**.'

To find the answer to an information retrieval question it is very important to look for the words from the question in the text. Look at the passage and question below:

What caused the boy to **fall off his bike**?

As the boy zoomed down the hill he felt the wind in his hair and the cool air on his face. He wanted the moment to last forever. Suddenly he caught sight of something out of the corner of his eye. He looked over his shoulder to see what it was and straight away he lost his balance and **fell off his bike**.

The last sentence of the passage is where you find the words **fell off his bike**, so this should tell you that the answer to the question lies within this sentence or very nearby.

In this case, your answer should be:

The boy fell off his bike because he looked over his shoulder and lost his balance.

Sometimes, the question is made slightly more difficult because the word used in the question and the word used in the text are different but they mean the same thing. For example, the word 'bicycle' or 'cycle' could be used in the passage, but the word 'bike' could be used in the question.

Another example is if you are asked what the weather was like, you might look for different weather words in the text, such as rain, wind, storm, even though the precise word 'weather' may not be found.

Train

Ellie had gone into the church because of her feet. This was not the best reason for entering a church, but Ellie was plump and middle-aged and her feet were hurting her. They were hurting her badly.

It was a beautiful sunny day in June and Ellie and her friend Sigrid (who was as thin as 5 Ellie was portly) had set out early from Vienna in the little train which took them up the mountains, so they could climb up to the top of a peak called the Dorfelspitze.

They went to the mountains on the last Sunday of every month, which was their day off, changing their aprons for dirndls and filling their rucksacks with salami sandwiches and slices of plum cake, so that when they got to the top they could admire the view without 10 getting hungry. It was how they refreshed their souls after the hard work they did all week, cleaning and cooking and shopping and scrubbing for the professors who employed them, and who were fussy about how things were done. Ellie was the cook and Sigrid was the housemaid and they had been friends for many years.

From *Journey to the River Sea*, Eva Ibbotson

1 Use the information in the extract above to answer the questions.

(a) Why did Ellie go into the church?

(b) What time of year is it in the passage?

(c) Where had Ellie and Sigrid set out from?

(d) On which specific day did the women go to the mountains?

(e) What did the women have in their rucksacks?

(f) Name two of the tasks that Ellie and Sigrid had to do for their employers.

Sometimes the question asks you to answer 'in your own words'. Then it is important that you do exactly that. You must not copy directly from the text as you will not gain any marks for this. Use different words that mean the same thing (synonyms) but do not change the meaning of what was in the text.

Test

Test time: 05:00

The enormous sandy beach was peppered with broken mussel shells, pebbles, seaweed and driftwood. There were red, yellow and blue umbrellas and stripy deck chairs lining the shoreline.

2 Describe the beach in your own words. (4)

Using inference and deduction

Skill definition: Understanding what you have read by drawing inferences, making deductions and justifying your choices with evidence.

Inference and deduction questions require you to give answers based on the information in the text but they are trickier because the answer will not be there in black and white. You will need to think like a detective. Piece together the clues in the text, and use your knowledge of how people think as well as your understanding of the world around you to help you to answer the questions.

Understanding the questions

In both inference and deduction questions you will often find the words 'do you think ...'. This is because there is not necessarily one right or wrong answer, so the examiner is looking for evidence that you can think independently and make connections between what you are reading and your knowledge of the world around you.

You will also often be asked to give *evidence* to support your answer in this type of question. As long as you have provided evidence that clearly supports your answer, you are likely to earn the marks even if it is different from someone else's.

Looking for clues in the text

Deduction questions ask you to work out some information from the clues in the text. There are hints that you need to collect together to work out an answer.

Text:	Looking out of the window, Hiruni decided that she'd had enough of being indoors. She was fed up of playing with her dolls. They were no fun anymore and she certainly didn't want to play with her brother. She cast her eyes towards the huge garden. It was like a jungle out there and she couldn't wait to explore. Without a second thought, Hiruni pulled on her wellington boots and hurried out to play.
Question:	What was the weather like that day?
Answer:	It was a rainy day. We know this because the character is putting on her wellington boots and she would only need these on a wet day.

Always remember that the answer to an inference question is somewhere in the text – it just won't be as obvious as for a retrieval question. You need to look for clues and put the pieces of the puzzle together.

1 Identify the key words in the question, e.g. weather in the example above.
2 Consider what kind of clues there might be that are related to the key words, e.g. types of weather, weather-specific clothing, reactions to weather (shivering, sweating, etc.).
3 Put the clues together to identify a type of weather that they point to.

You may have to deduce information about characters.

Text: Cassie and Selena walked into the classroom together but that was the end of their interaction. As usual, Cassie strode straight to the back row, slumping in a chair after dumping her books on the desk with a thud. She was quickly surrounded by a group of similarly disinterested friends. Selena cautiously chose a seat in the front and laid out her books and pencils neatly, trying to ignore the giggles from the back row.

Question: Are Cassie and Selena friends?

Answer: No they are not. Although they walk in together, they don't sit together, they clearly have different attitudes to school and it is suggested that Cassie and her friends are laughing at Selena.

Forming opinions based on the text

Inference questions are different from deduction as they ask for an opinion based on the clues, rather than a fact. You need to consider a range of evidence in the text, look at it together and form an opinion that is logical and rational based on the clues.

Again, consider a range of evidence based on the key word in the question. In the example below you are being asked about how Tim feels so look for:

- emotion words
- actions that show emotion, e.g. crying
- ways of speaking, e.g. sobbed, murmured.

Then think of a way to describe how he is feeling, using your own words. This links to the skill of summarising.

> You are often asked to 'refer to the text', 'give evidence' or 'use quotations' in your answer. Pick short examples from the text that were the clues you found to create your answer.

Tim opened the door cautiously, trying not to make a sound. He tiptoed over the threshold, quivering slightly, his heart beating hard in his chest. His hands shook as he pulled the door behind him and he bolted down the path to safety.

Question: How is Tim feeling at this moment? Refer to the text in your answer. (4)

Answer: Tim is nervous and afraid. The fact that he opens the door 'cautiously' shows he is unsure and his 'quivering' and 'heart beating hard' show that he is afraid. The mention of 'safety' at the end suggests that he was unsafe before this moment.

> When you are answering an inference or deduction question, you may find it useful to use the sentence opener 'This suggests ...'. When there is more than one possible answer, you are not expected to make definite statements. It is fine to use conditional language, including 'may', 'might' and 'perhaps' to express your thoughts.

1 Read the passage below and answer the questions.

As Ellen entered the park she could smell the fresh scent of the newly cut grass. She breathed it in deeply and smiled. All around her, the shoots of daffodils and snowdrops were appearing through the soil and the baby birds were tweeting in the treetops. She laid out her picnic blanket and took her sketchbook from her backpack. She marvelled at the nature around her as she began to put pencil to paper.

(a) What time of the year is it in this passage?

(b) Do you think Ellen is enjoying being in the park? Give evidence to support your answer.

Test   Test time: 10:00

2 Read the following text carefully and then answer the questions that follow.

As he dragged himself out of the water and hauled his weary bones on to the sandy shore, Sanjit's mind was whirling. How had he arrived here? Why couldn't he remember what had happened? And most importantly, where *was* he? Sanjit's muscles screamed with pain and his eyes stung as he lay spread-eagled on his back. His entire body was a
5 patchwork of green and purple and as the sun beat down on him the pain grew more and more intense. Sanjit willed himself to remember. Where had he been? What had he been doing? How had he ended up here? Carefully he uncurled his left hand and stared in confusion at the small gold key that lay on his palm.

(a) What do you think is the 'patchwork' referred to in the text?   (1)

(b) What kind of story do you think this is? Give evidence to support your answer.   (2)

(c) How do you think Sanjit is feeling? Use phrases from the text to support your answer. (3)

Making predictions

Skill definition: Predicting what might happen in a text, using details both stated and implied.

You may be asked to predict what will happen next in a text, either by explaining your prediction or by writing the next paragraph (or more) of the story. This skill is a type of inference question as you must use the text as a basis for your ideas.

Clues provided by the author

Good authors sometimes use your desire to predict what might happen next using a technique called 'foreshadowing'. This is an advance signal of what could happen in the future and is used to give readers clues about what will occur later in the story. For example, a character hears a door slam in an empty house and puts it down to a draught; in the next chapter a ghost appears in their bedroom.

These clues might be accurate or they might be misleading if the author wants to trick you into thinking something will happen when he or she knows that is not the case.

Understanding the questions

In a comprehension test, you will sometimes be expected to predict what might happen next. You will not necessarily see the word 'predict' in the question, but in some exams you may be asked to write the next one or two paragraphs of the story using a style similar to the author's. These questions are often the last question in the test and are worth a significant number of marks. In order to gain these marks it is important that you have thought carefully about what you have read and looked for clues.

Train •••••••••••••••••••••••••••••••••

1 Here are some common examples of foreshadowing that are used in literature. Try to match each example with the event that happens later in the story:

Events in the text	Prediction
A A man goes off to war and tells his wife and children that he will be home before they know it.	1 The characters will get hopelessly lost.
B A girl meets a boy and her parents disapprove of him.	2 The character will become very ill.
C A character complains of a headache but is told that it is 'nothing'.	3 The characters will fall in love.
D A husband tells his wife that it is fine to leave their son on his own for five minutes.	4 The character will die.
E A father tells his children that of course they won't need a map.	5 The character will break something expensive.

Read the following chapter ending from *Dolphin Song* by Lauren St John.

Dolphin Song is about an eleven-year-old orphan called Martine who lives with her grandmother on a game reserve in South Africa. Martine makes friends with a white giraffe and discovers that she has a secret talent for healing animals. At this point in the story, Martine's class is on a school trip to the islands of Mozambique to witness the legendary 'Sardine Run' but one night there is a terrible storm and the children find themselves shipwrecked on an island. They have just discovered a fresh-water lake.

Martine, who'd been so eager for a drink and a bath that she'd been poised to leap into the shallows, fully-clothed, decided that cleanliness was not a priority after all. She'd had enough problems with sharks; she didn't need new nightmares about crocodiles. 'Maybe I've had enough of being in water for the time being …' she began.

5 She stopped. Ben was holding his nose.

'Okay, I take the hint,' she said crossly, 'but if I get attacked by a crocodile, you're going to have to answer to my grandmother.'

As soon as the words were out, it hit her that she'd been so preoccupied with searching for Ben and thinking about how hungry she was and how much her head hurt, she hadn't

10 taken in that there was no guarantee she would see her grandmother or her beloved white giraffe ever again. It was heart-breaking to realize that her grandmother's last memory of her might be of their fight, and that Jemmy would never understand that something had happened to prevent her returning to him. He'd think she'd abandoned him.

Ben saw the anguish on her face and his own sobered. 'Listen, if there's a way off this

15 island, we'll find it, I promise. You *will* see your grandmother and Jemmy again, and I *will* see my mum and dad. But I have a feeling that the dolphins have brought us here for a reason. It's up to us to figure out what that reason might be.'

2 Give an example from the text that shows that the story is set in Africa. (1)

3 What genre do you think this story belongs to? Explain your answer, giving evidence from the text. (3)

4 How do you think this story will end? Predict what might happen in the rest of the story, based on what you have read. You should aim to write a paragraph explaining how you think the story will continue and eventually end, remembering to support your ideas with close reference to the text. (6)

Separating fact and opinion in non-fiction texts

Skill definition: Distinguishing between statements of fact and opinion.

When you are given a non-fiction text in a comprehension test, it is important to think carefully about how much truth lies behind the words you are reading. Many examples of non-fiction writing include elements of both fact and opinion, and it is the balance between these two elements that can help the reader work out the purpose of the text.

It is a good idea to begin by deciding which type of text you are reading to give you some idea as to how much of the content is likely to be the author's personal opinion.

Texts that are likely to be factual

- In an **explanation** text or a **report**, most of the text consists of facts because the purpose of the text is to inform the reader, so the writer doesn't need to include many of their own opinions.

Texts containing a balanced view

- The most obvious type of text giving a balanced view is a **discursive** text. These texts give two sides of an argument, offering equal amounts of information to support both viewpoints.
- Newspaper articles should also provide a balanced view. In theory, a newspaper article should be impersonal and unbiased (not taking sides) in its approach, so the only statements that are likely to be opinions are those within 'speech marks' or 'inverted commas'.

Texts that are likely to show bias

- Biased texts include **biography**, **autobiography** and **letters**.
- **Persuasive** writing is also heavily biased as the purpose of a persuasive text is to convince the reader to do or think something. The writing is likely to include some statements of fact but a significant proportion of the text will consist of the writer's opinions.

Think about where the information comes from when deciding what is fact and what is opinion.

Fact

- Statistics from reputable sources, for example, 'According to a national survey, 75 per cent of people in the UK are worried about the effects of global warming.'
- Unbiased **report** or **recount** of real events, for example, 'Reporters heard the explosion at 12.35 p.m.'
- Proven statements, for example, 'The Met Office measured the lowest temperature at −17 degrees.'

Opinion

- Quotes from non-experts, for example, '"I believe that most people worry about global warming," said the head teacher.'
- Opinions and suppositions, for example, 'Witnesses suggested that the explosion was caused by a gas leak.'
- Unproven statements or guesses, for example, 'A local resident in Glasgow said, "I reckon it was the coldest day of the year yesterday."'

1   Identify the key word (or words) in each sentence that shows if it is fact or opinion.

    (a) Most people believe that smoking should be illegal.

    (b) The Office for National Statistics reported that in 2014, crime fell by 8 per cent.

    (c) It was the view of the residents that the new road would cause more pollution.

    (d) Experts suspect that a cure will be found soon.

> A fact should be able to be proved. An opinion lacks evidence and is just what somebody thinks – they do not know for sure and others may disagree.

2   Read the following text and identify all the facts and all the opinions:

> A baby girl had a very lucky escape after falling 250ft down a ravine in the back of a runaway four-wheel-drive vehicle in France.
>
> Brian Thompson, 38, and his wife Barbara, 35, had stopped to take photographs next to the Pont de Terenez suspension bridge near Crozon in Brittany when their Nissan Qashqai
> 5   sped, out of control, down an embankment with their three-month-old daughter, Lucinda, in the child-safety seat.
>
> Mr Thompson, a teacher from Southfield, North-east London, said: "I was sure that she would not have survived the fall. We both were. It was the most terrifying experience of my life."
>
> Miraculously, Lucinda escaped with just a couple of scratches on her face and a bruised
> 10   right arm. "When I looked through the window and saw her looking at me, I don't mind admitting that I burst into tears. It was a miracle," said Mr Thompson.
>
> The vehicle, which was written off in the accident, came to a halt just inches away from a fast-flowing river and had smoke pouring from the engine.
>
> An investigation is now underway into what went wrong. Mr Thompson said, "The
> 15   handbrake was on when the Qashqai was at the top of the ravine, and it was still on when it was at the bottom."
>
> Earlier that day, Mr and Mrs Thompson had called into a local church to light a candle. Mrs Thompson said: "Going into that church was a blessing. My mother often used to tell me that I should light a candle whenever I visit a church. The angels must have been
> 20   watching over my daughter today."

Test   Test time: 15:00

Use the text above to answer the following questions.

3   What does Mr Thompson's statement 'It was a miracle' tell us about his view of events?   (2)

4   Rewrite this sentence as part of the article, rather than a quotation:

    "I was sure that she would not have survived the fall. We both were. It was the most terrifying experience of my life."   (2)

5   In your opinion, does this newspaper article give a balanced or a biased view? Explain your answer carefully using evidence from the text.   (3)

Analysing language

Skill definition: Understanding, demonstrating and evaluating how or why a writer uses language. Analysing the effect that language has upon the reader.

The language that writers use is very important. The words and techniques they choose have a huge impact on the reader. Not only do they help the reader to picture the scenes and characters involved, but they also create a particular atmosphere or mood, or guide the reader's feelings about characters and events. A high number of marks are often available for questions involving the language the writer uses.

Verbs

At a very basic level, the verb choices that the writer makes have a huge impact. Read the following passage and think about the atmosphere that is created and what you find out about Maria:

Maria <u>stormed</u> out of the house, <u>kicking</u> the flowers as she <u>stomped</u> down the path. When she reached Louisa's house she <u>flung</u> open the back door and <u>burst</u> in.

There is no mention of Maria's mood, but the underlined verbs clearly convey a sense of anger and annoyance. If the verbs were changed, the atmosphere of the piece would be very different.

Train ●

1   Write an alternative version of this text using different verbs that create a different atmosphere. You could think about creating a spooky atmosphere or a happy atmosphere, for example.

Descriptive language

The use of descriptive words, especially adjectives, contributes enormously to the reader's understanding of characters. Look carefully at the following short passages from *The Lives of Christopher Chant* by Diana Wynne Jones:

There was a new governess sitting on the only <u>hard</u> chair, wearing the usual sort of <u>ugly</u> greyish clothes and a hat that was uglier than usual. Her drab cotton gloves were folded on her <u>dull</u> bag and her head hung down as if she were timid or put-upon, or both.

The passage introduces the governess and the reader gets a clear impression of the narrator's feelings towards her from the use of the underlined adjectives. It is obvious that the governess is an unexciting character from the dreary, boring language.

> ... he was wearing tweeds, strong and tangy and almost fox-coloured, which were a little baggy here and there, but blended beautifully with the darker foxiness of Uncle Ralph's hair and the redder foxiness of his moustache ... As a final touch, Uncle Ralph smiled at him like sunlight on an autumn forest.
>
> From *The Lives of Christopher Chant* by Diana Wynne Jones

2   What impression do you get about Uncle Ralph in the passage above? Refer to the language used.

Understanding questions involving verb choice and descriptive language

Language analysis questions will often ask you to support your answers with evidence.

There is very rarely an absolute right or wrong answer to a question about language. If you make sensible points, support them with evidence and explain them, you will earn the marks. A very good format to use is the **Point, Evidence, Explanation** (PEE) format. Here is an example of a question, showing how marks would be allocated based on PEE:

> This text is taken from a book called *Mortlock* by Jon Mayhew. The book is about two orphaned children who discover they have a shared past. One day this past comes back to haunt them and forces them to run for their lives.

> Thorns and briars snagged and tore at them, ripping flesh and clothes as they fought their way through the vegetation. Mortlock could hear Corvis panting up ahead ... Cold fingers raked his shoulders and snagged at his hair; the sweet stench of decay clogged his nostrils. He slashed at the limbs that tried to snare him, shuddering as his fingers brushed against dry, icy skin.

What type of atmosphere has the author created in this passage?   (3)

(POINT)

3-mark answer: In this passage the author has created a frightening atmosphere. He does this using

(EVIDENCE)

verbs like 'ripping' and 'slashed' and adjectives including 'cold' and 'icy'. The verbs make it seem as

(EXPLANATION)

though something dangerous is happening and the adjectives have a chilling effect, which makes the reader feel afraid.

3 Read the opening to Chapter 4 of Michael Morpurgo's *Kensuke's Kingdom*. Identify any information that relates to the mood or atmosphere.

(4)

> The terrors came fast, one upon another. The lights of the *Peggy Sue* went away into the dark of the night, leaving me alone in the ocean, alone with the certainty that they were already too far away, that my cries for help could not possibly be heard. I thought then of the sharks cruising the black water beneath me – scenting me, already searching me out,
> 5 homing in on me – and I knew there could be no hope. I would be eaten alive. Either that or I would drown slowly. Nothing could save me.
> I trod water, frantically searching the impenetrable darkness about me for something, anything to swim towards. There was nothing.

Figurative language techniques

Use of words or phrases that describe one thing in terms of another is called figurative language. It often uses comparisons to create a vivid picture in the reader's mind – this may also be referred to as **imagery** as it creates an image for the reader. It is not meant to be understood literally but requires the reader to use the comparison to help them understand what the writer means. Figurative language involves an imaginative comparison between seemingly unlikely things. It may also use sound to add to a description.

As you read the examples below, think about the effect that each technique has on the reader.

● **Similes**: comparing something to something else, using 'like' or 'as … as'

Her eyes were like emeralds.

● **Metaphors**: saying something *is* something else

His legs were matchsticks.

● **Personification**: making something that is not human seem human

The mist embraced the trees.

When you are reading any text in an exam, it is also important to look out for other descriptive techniques, including:

● **Onomatopoeia**: using words that sound like the noises they describe

pop, fizz, crash

● **Alliteration**: repeating the same letter or sound at the beginning of two or more words in a sentence or line

The wind whispers through the weeping willows.

● **Repetition**: repeating a word, phrase or idea for effect

Understanding questions involving figurative language

These techniques are used in many different types of writing, but they are particularly common in poetry, where words are limited. Look at the following annotated extract from 'The Eagle' by Alfred Lord Tennyson.

> He clasps the crag with crooked hands; — Alliteration, hard 'c'
> — Personification
> Close to the sun in lonely lands, — Alliteration, soft 'l'
> Ringed with the azure world, he stands. — Personification
>
> — Metaphor
> The wrinkled sea beneath him crawls; — Personification
> He watches from his mountain walls, — Simile
> And like a thunderbolt he falls.

How has the author portrayed the eagle in this poem? (6)

A model answer may include the following points:

● The use of alliteration and the repetition of the hard 'c' sound in the first line gives a sense of the harsh environment that the eagle lives in.
● The use of personification, where the poet gives the eagle 'hands' like a human, makes him seem powerful.
● The soft 'l' sound in the second line makes the eagle seem very solitary and independent – he does not need anyone or anything else so he lives in 'lonely lands'.
● The use of the phrase 'he stands' rather than 'he perches' in the third line, makes the eagle seem majestic and powerful.
● The metaphor 'wrinkled sea' gives a sense of how high the eagle is above the ground – the sea is so small that it looks wrinkled, which is a word we usually associate with smaller things.
● The personification of the sea, that 'crawls' makes the eagle seem more powerful and more important – it can move much faster than the slow, crawling sea.
● The simile in the last line, comparing the eagle to a 'thunderbolt' makes the eagle seem immensely powerful and almost god-like.

It is very important to be specific when you answer this type of question. You need to refer to the particular words in the phrase and describe why you think the author has chosen that particular comparison. Consider each word and what you associate with that word. For example, 'like a thunderbolt' – thunderbolts are fast and powerful so the eagle seems faster and more powerful.

● Generalisations like 'the simile makes the poem more vivid' or 'the use of personification has a better effect on the reader' will not gain you any marks.

> It is important that you are familiar with all the techniques listed on page 73 and their definitions. In a question about use of language, you should identify the techniques and describe how and why they are used.

Find out about how to use descriptive language in your own writing on pages 110–111.

Train

4 Read the following passage from *Wolf Brother* by Michele Paver, then identify words, phrases and techniques that the author has used to make the reader feel tense.

> Again the Forest shook. The trees tensed to listen. But this time Torak realised that the roars were far away: many daywalks to the west. Slowly he breathed out.
>
> At the mouth of the shelter, the cub sat watching him. Its slanted eyes were a strange, dark gold. Amber, thought Torak, remembering the little seal amulet that Fa had worn on a
> 5 thong around his neck.
>
> He found that oddly reassuring. At least he wasn't alone.
>
> As his heartbeats returned to normal, the pain of his fever came surging back. It crisped his skin. His skull felt ready to burst. He struggled to get more willow bark from his medicine pouch, but dropped it, and couldn't find it again in the half-darkness. He dragged
> 10 another branch onto the fire, then lay back, gasping.
>
> He couldn't get those roars out of his head. Where was the bear now?

Notice that this text also contains different sentence structures to build the tension: short sentences, e.g. 'Again the Forest shook'; questions, e.g. 'Where was the bear now?'. To learn about how to improve your writing using different sentence structures go to pages 114–115.

Test

Test time: 15:00

Read the following text carefully and then answer the questions that follow:

> But on she went, pulling herself up now and again by rooty stems into this jungle of moss and wood-violet and creeping leaves of clover. The sharp-seeming grass blades, waist high, were tender to the touch and sprang back lightly behind her as she passed. When at last she reached the foot of the tree, the bird took fright and flew away and she sat down
> 5 suddenly on a gnarled leaf of primrose. The air was filled with scent. 'But nothing will play with you,' she thought and saw the cracks and furrows of the primrose leaves held crystal beads of dew. If she pressed the leaf these rolled like marbles.
>
> The bank was warm, almost too warm here within the shelter of the tall grass, and the sandy earth smelled dry. Standing up, she picked a primrose. The pink stalk felt tender and
> 10 living in her hands and was covered with silvery hairs, and when she held the flower, like a parasol, between her eyes and the sky, she saw the sun's pale light through the veined petals.
>
> On a piece of bark she found a wood-louse and she struck it lightly with her swaying flower. It curled immediately and became a ball, bumping softly away downhill in amongst the grass roots.
>
> From *The Borrowers* by Mary Norton

5 What is the effect of the metaphor used in the opening sentence? (1)

6 In this extract the author uses language to emphasise how small the child is. Give an example and explain how it shows this. (2)

7 Choose two examples of figurative language used in this extract and explain their effects. (4)

Test 2: Fiction comprehension

You should aim to complete this test in 45 minutes. Spend 10 minutes reading the article and the questions and then 35 minutes answering the questions.

This extract is taken from the opening chapters of *The Mourning Emporium* by Michelle Lovric. The book is about two children called Teo and Renzo who are battling against the evil spirit of Bajamonte Tiepolo and his ambitions to destroy Venice and all things Venice-related.

Venice, late afternoon, Christmas Day, 1900

A small girl stood on the ice that crusted the edge of the lagoon. The storm was over. But the temperature was still falling. The girl shivered, wrapping her arms around her narrow body.

This was not the kind of cold that makes your nose glow, nor the kind that makes you look forward to sitting by the fire with a nice warm cup of something. It was that hopeless,
5   heart-dragging kind of cold that makes you feel like an orphan.

Particularly if you are one.

Like this girl, Teodora Gasperin.

As far as the eye could see, way out on the islands of the lagoon, droplets of fog had frozen into a crystalline haze over the skeletal branches of the trees. It looked as if the
10 leaves had been replaced by diamonds, glittering like angry teardrops. Ice strangled the shore; long white arabesques of it reached into the black water.

As she turned to trudge back home, Teo's eye snagged on something glinting just below her, embedded in the frozen water. She bent down, lifting her pinafore out of the way for a better look.

15 Then she screamed.

For what she had glimpsed was a white eel, thick and long as a young tree trunk, with red gills sprouting like coral from its muscular neck. At the sound of her cry, the creature slowly lowered one translucent eyelid and winked at her.

"Vampire Eels!" Teo shuddered. "They're back." And Venice all but drowned under the
20 ice. It could only mean one thing.

"Renzo!" she whispered to herself. "I must tell Renzo! And the mermaids. And Professor Marin and the other *Incogniti* …"

A black-backed gull flapped past, cawing "Ha! Ha! Ha!"

Teo winced at its mockery. Her nose pinkened, and she blinked rapidly. Then she
25 stamped her foot.

"Yes, I know. I know. I *know*. If Bajamonte Tiepolo has come back, and brought all his vile creatures with him, and baddened magic too, then there's only one person to blame."

The girl lifted her head and cried out over the icy tracts: "Me."

Osborne House, the Isle of Wight, Christmas Day, 1900

When the news of the disaster was brought to Queen Victoria, she did not lift her
30 dimming eyes from the soft-boiled egg in her golden egg-cup.

"Venice?" she frowned.

"The island city, Ma'am. In Italy, Ma'am – it has been destroyed, they say."

"Is this Ve…?" The Queen stopped, her lip trembling.

"Venice, Ma'am," the nurse reminded her gently.

35 "… a part of Our Empire?"

"No, Ma'am, Venice has never been one of ours. Won't you try a little egg? It is exceedingly lightly done."

A sudden shadow darkened the window. A cormorant stood motionless on the sill, its ink-black wings spread out.

40 "Another one!" the nurse grimaced. "I do so hate those birds. Uncannily like bats, they are." She turned back to her patient, "Now, Ma'am …"

But the Queen had fallen asleep again, the teaspoon still clutched in her tiny, wrinkled hand.

1 What is the weather like at the beginning of the story? (1)

2 What atmosphere has the author created in the first two paragraphs? Give evidence to support your answer. (3)

3 What is the effect of the phrase 'skeletal branches of the trees'? (2)

4 Explain in your own words what happens when Teo looks into the lagoon. (3)

5 How does the nurse's language and behaviour suggest that she respects the Queen? (2)

6 What effect does the appearance of the cormorant have on the reader? (2)

7 What impression of the Queen is conveyed by the phrase 'the teaspoon still clutched in her tiny, wrinkled hand.' (2)

8 What impression do you get of Teo from the first chapter? Support your answer with close reference to the text. (4)

9 Give definitions for the following words: crystalline; embedded; pinafore; uncannily. (4)

10 What links the two opening chapters? (1)

   A They are both about the same characters.

   B They are both set in the same country.

   C They both take place on the same day.

   D They both feature eels.

   E They are both the same length.

11 'Ice strangled the shore' is an example of which technique? (1)

   A alliteration

   B simile

   C onomatopoeia

   D repetition

   E personification

12 The author uses the simile 'thick and long as a young tree trunk' to describe the eel. What does this suggest about the eel? (1)

   A It is strong and full of life.

   B It is tall and green.

   C It is made of wood.

   D It is covered in leaves.

   E It is going to kill Teo.

13 How do you think Teo is feeling, when the author writes 'she turned to trudge home'? (1)

  A   happy

  B   confident

  C   energetic

  D   down-hearted

  E   ill

14 Which word or phrase suggests that the Queen is going blind? (1)

  A   'her lip trembling'

  B   'she frowned'

  C   'her dimming eyes'

  D   'A sudden shadow'

  E   'the nurse grimaced'

15 Which of the following is an opinion, rather than a fact? (1)

  A   'A small girl stood on the ice'

  B   'there's only one person to blame'

  C   'news of the disaster was brought to Queen Victoria'

  D   'The girl shivered'

  E   'Her nose pinkened'

Record your score and time here and at the start of the book.

Score ☐ / 29   Time ☐ : ☐

Test 3: Non-fiction comprehension

You should aim to complete this test in 45 minutes. Spend 10 minutes reading the passage and the questions and then 35 minutes answering the questions.

This extract is taken from the prologue of *Notes from a Small Island* by Bill Bryson. The passage describes this American writer's arrival in England for the very first time.

My first sight of England was on a foggy March night in 1973 when I arrived on the midnight ferry from Calais. For twenty minutes, the terminal area was aswarm with activity as cars and lorries poured forth, customs people did their duties, and everyone made for the London road. Then abruptly all was silence and I wandered through sleeping,

5 low-lit streets threaded with fog, just like in a Bulldog Drummond movie. It was rather wonderful having an English town all to myself.

The only mildly dismaying thing was that all the hotels and guesthouses appeared to be shut up for the night. I walked as far as the rail station, thinking I'd catch a train to London, but the station, too, was dark and shuttered. I was standing wondering what to do when

10 I noticed a grey light of television filling an upstairs window of a guesthouse across the road. Hooray, I thought, someone awake, and hastened across, planning humble apologies to the kindly owner for the lateness of my arrival and imagining a cheery conversation which included the line, "Oh, but I couldn't possibly ask you to feed me at this hour. No, honestly well, if you're quite sure it's no trouble, then perhaps just a roast beef sandwich

15 and a large dill pickle with perhaps some potato salad and a bottle of beer." The front path was pitch dark and in my eagerness and unfamiliarity with British doorways, I tripped on a step, crashing face-first into the door and sending half a dozen empty milk bottles clattering. Almost immediately the upstairs window opened.

"Who's that?" came a sharp voice.

20 I stepped back, rubbing my nose, and peered up at a silhouette with hair curlers. "Hello, I'm looking for a room," I said.

"We're shut."

"Oh." But what about my supper?

"Try the Churchill. On the front."

25 "On the front of what?" I asked, but the window was already banging closed.

The Churchill was sumptuous and well lit and appeared ready to receive visitors. Through a window I could see people in suits in a bar, looking elegant and suave, like characters from a Noel Coward play. I hesitated in the shadows, feeling like a street urchin. I was socially and sartorially ill-suited for such an establishment and anyway it was clearly

30 beyond my meagre budget. Only the previous day, I had handed over an exceptionally plump wad of colourful francs to a beady-eyed Picardy hotelier in payment for one night in a lumpy bed and a plate of mysterious chasseur containing the bones of assorted small animals, much of which had to be secreted away in a large napkin in order not to appear impolite, and had determined thenceforth to be more cautious with expenditures. So

35 I turned reluctantly from the Churchill's beckoning warmth and trudged off into the darkness.

Further along Marine Parade stood a shelter, open to the elements but roofed, and I decided that this was as good as I was going to get. With my backpack for a pillow, I lay down and drew my jacket tight around me. The bench was slatted and hard and studded

40 with big round-headed bolts that made reclining in comfort an impossibility and doubtless
their intention. I lay for a long time listening to the sea washing over the shingle below,
and eventually dropped off to a long, cold night of mumbled dreams in which I found
myself being pursued over Arctic ice floes by a beady-eyed Frenchman with a catapult, a
bag of bolts, and an uncanny aim, who thwacked me repeatedly in the buttocks and legs
45 for stealing a linen napkin full of seepy food and leaving it at the back of a dresser drawer
of my hotel room. I awoke with a gasp about three, stiff all over and quivering from cold.
The fog had gone. The air was now still and clear, and the sky was bright with stars. A
beacon from the lighthouse at the far end of the breakwater swept endlessly over the sea.
It was all most fetching, but I was far too cold to appreciate it. I dug shiveringly through
50 my backpack and extracted every potentially warming item I could find – a flannel shirt,
two sweaters, an extra pair of jeans. I used some woollen socks as mittens and put a pair of
flannel boxer shorts on my head as a kind of desperate headwarmer, then sank heavily back
onto the bench and waited patiently for death's sweet kiss. Instead, I fell asleep.

1 What was worrying the writer when he first arrived in England? (1)

2 In paragraph 1, what impression does the narrator have of Britain? (2)

3 Explain in your own words, how the narrator is made to seem clumsy in paragraph 2. (2)

4 Explain what is meant by the phrase 'On the front' and why this is confusing for the
narrator. (2)

5 How does the narrator's expectation of the hotel owner compare to the reality? Give
evidence from the passage to support your answer. (4)

6 Summarise the narrator's overall opinion of his earlier stay in France. Refer to the text
in your answer. (4)

7 Why do you think the narrator dreams about the Arctic? (2)

8 How does the narrator feel about sleeping outside? Give evidence to support your answer. (2)

9 Why does the narrator use the phrase 'death's sweet kiss' in the final paragraph? (2)

10 Of which technique is the following sentence an example 'I wandered through sleeping,
low-lit streets'? (1)

   A metaphor

   B repetition

   C onomatopoeia

   D personification

   E simile

11 Which of the following adjectives is not associated with the Churchill or its guests? (1)

   A sumptuous

   B elegant

   C ill-suited

   D suave

   E beckoning

12 Which phrase suggests that the narrator is sad to leave the Churchill? (1)

   A 'feeling like a street urchin'

   B 'sumptuous and well lit'

   C 'I was socially and sartorially ill-suited'

   D 'I turned reluctantly'

   E 'I hesitated in the shadows'

13 Which of the following words best suggests that Marine Parade was a pleasant place? (1)

   A slatted

   B fetching

   C quivering

   D shingle

   E breakwater

14 Which of the following statements from the passage is an opinion? (1)

   A 'customs people did their duties'

   B 'I walked as far as the rail station'

   C 'I awoke with a gasp'

   D 'the upstairs window opened'

   E 'this was as good as I was going to get'

15 From your reading of the passage, which of the following events do you think is most likely to happen next? (1)

   A the narrator will die

   B the narrator will go straight back to America

   C the narrator will wake up in discomfort

   D the narrator will go for a swim

   E the narrator will wake up in a hotel

Record your score and time here and at the start of the book.

Score ☐ / 27 Time ☐ : ☐

Test 4: Poetry comprehension

You should aim to complete this test in 45 minutes. Spend 10 minutes reading the poem and the questions and then 35 minutes answering the questions.

This extract is from *The Rime of the Ancient Mariner* by Samuel Taylor Coleridge. This narrative poem was written in 1797 and tells the story of a sailor who once went on an extraordinary journey.

    The ship was cheer'd, the harbour clear'd,
    Merrily did we drop
    Below the kirk, below the hill,
    Below the lighthouse top.

5   The Sun came up upon the left,
    Out of the sea came he!
    And he shone bright and on the right
    Went down into the sea.

    Higher and higher every day,
10   Till over the mast at noon –
    The Wedding-Guest here beat his breast,
    For he heard the loud bassoon.

    The bride hath paced into the hall,
    Red as a rose is she;
15   Nodding their heads before her goes
    The merry minstrelsy.

    The Wedding-Guest he beat his breast,
    Yet he cannot choose but hear;
    And thus spake on that ancient man,
20   The bright-eyed Mariner.

    And now the Storm-blast came, and he
    Was tyrannous and strong:
    He struck with his o'ertaking wings,
    And chased us south along.

25   With sloping masts and dipping prow,
    As who pursued with yell and blow
    Still treads the shadow of his foe,
    And forward bends his head,
    The ship drove fast, loud roar'd the blast,
30   And southward aye we fled.

And now there came both mist and snow,
And it grew wondrous cold:
And ice, mast-high, came floating by,
As green as emerald.

35 And through the drifts the snowy clifts
Did send a dismal sheen:
Nor shapes of men nor beasts we ken –
The ice was all between.

The ice was here, the ice was there,
40 The ice was all around:
It crack'd and growl'd, and roar'd and howl'd,
Like noises in a swound!

At length did cross an Albatross,
Thorough the fog it came;
45 As if it had been a Christian soul,
We hail'd it in God's name.

It ate the food it ne'er had eat,
And round and round it flew.
The ice did split with a thunder-fit;
50 The helmsman steer'd us through.

And a good south wind sprung up behind;
The Albatross did follow,
And every day, for food or play,
Came to the mariners' hollo!

55 In mist or cloud, on mast or shroud,
It perch'd for vespers nine;
Whiles all the night, through fog-smoke white,
Glimmer'd the white moonshine.

'God save thee, ancient Mariner,
60 From the fiends, that plague thee thus! –
Why look'st thou so?' – With my crossbow
I shot the Albatross

1 On which side of the ship does the sun rise? (1)
2 Find and copy the simile in stanza 4 and explain why you think the author chose it. (3)
3 Who is listening to the mariner's story? (1)
4 Explain in your own words what happens in stanza 8. (3)
5 In modern English, give two of the noises the ice makes in stanza 10. (2)
6 What makes the wedding guest interrupt the mariner in the last stanza? (2)

7 Which of these places is *not* mentioned in the first stanza? (1)

   A the harbour

   B the lighthouse

   C the hall

   D the kirk

   E the hill

8 In stanza 6, how does the poet make the storm sound like it is alive? Refer to the text in your answer. (3)

9 What do you think the word 'helmsman' means? (1)

10 What colour was the ice? (1)

   A green

   B transparent

   C white

   D blue

   E yellow

11 How did the mariners treat the albatross when it first arrived? (1)

   A they shot it

   B they hailed it

   C they fed it

   D they threw things at it

   E they ate it

12 How does the poet make the ice seem frightening? Refer to the text in your answer. (4)

Record your score and time here and at the start of the book.

Score ☐ / 23 Time ☐ : ☐

3 Composition

Introduction

In your 11+ exam you will most likely have to complete a piece of writing. It might be a story, a diary entry, a speech, a book review or a response to a picture. Sometimes you are given a choice and, if so, this chapter will help you to choose which piece of writing to tackle (pages 87–88) and plan your writing (pages 89–91). The various types of composition are then considered in turn (see pages 92–104). Finally you will be given specific advice on how to improve your writing (pages 108–119).

The aim of this chapter is to give you the skills to pick up your pen and approach a wide range of writing tasks with confidence.

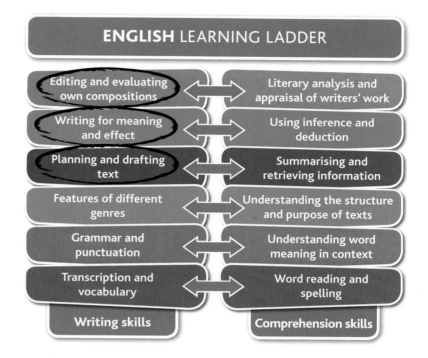

If you look at the left-hand side of the Learning Ladder, starting at the bottom, you will see that you have already stepped up the first three rungs: 'Transcription and vocabulary', 'Grammar and punctuation' and 'Features of different genres'. You are now going to take three more steps up the last three rungs: 'Planning and drafting text', 'Writing for meaning and effect' and then, finally, 'Editing and evaluating own compositions'.

When completing the tasks in this chapter, you will want to assess how well you have completed them. Use the success grids on pages 141–144, choosing the correct one for the given task. Composition marking is a subjective task and everyone will judge your piece slightly differently but the grids give a good starting point of what an examiner will be looking for. To get a balanced view, try asking a parent to assess your work, then assess it yourself. Use the grid to help you write a second improved draft.

Advice for parents

When marking a piece of writing, teachers and examiners know that working under timed conditions has an impact on the type of work children produce. However, there are certain things that candidates must do in order to satisfy the requirements of the senior school, so let us get into the mind of a marker and see what these things are.

First of all, has the child done as the question asked? You would be surprised how often children mis-read (or decide to ignore) the question. So, if asked for a **description** of a disused railway station, description should be the focus of the piece. It is no good writing two sentences about the station and then turning it into a story about a train crash. Not doing as the question asks can lose a lot of marks, so do encourage your child to make sure they follow the instructions provided.

Next, the marker is looking at the structure of the piece. To the trained and experienced eye it will be evident as to whether or not it has been planned so always encourage children to spend some time structuring their work before they start.

The marker next considers the writing itself. At the very least, it should consist of properly punctuated sentences. This is a basic requirement.

Spelling is then assessed. If your child finds spelling challenging but constructs words phonetically so that the meaning is reasonably clear, this is unlikely to be judged too harshly. High quality vocabulary will be more greatly rewarded than accurate spelling so encourage children to choose great words, even if a letter or two in them may be incorrect.

So a piece that does what the question says, is structured logically and written in properly punctuated sentences will do well. To do *very* well, you need to apply some of the features of language and structure considered later in this chapter. In order to award higher marks, examiners will be looking for a range of vocabulary, imagery, sentence structures and other writing features.

A word here about dyslexia and other learning difficulties. If your child has been diagnosed with a learning difficulty, please do not try to hide it from the senior school. It is far better to have this taken into account when the marking takes place.

Another well-meaning but potentially harmful thing that parents often do is to teach their child a string of long, poetic-sounding words and phrases, then issue strict instructions to include them in any written task. Children cannot keep up this sort of thing for long (thank goodness). A few sentences later they start to write in their true voice and it becomes clear to an examiner that they are not responding naturally to the task. Instead, if you want to help to broaden your child's vocabulary, try crosswords or word games such as those suggested below.

Word games

- Make lists of alternatives (synonyms) to verbs such as 'say' and 'walk'.
- Play alphabet games in which you name things from A to Z such as animals (antelope, bear, cheetah ... zebra), adverbs (anxiously, boringly, cunningly ... zanily) or food (avocado, beetroot, cheese ... zucchini) – all of these things get them thinking about words.
- Think of sentences in which the first word begins with a, the second with b and so on. (You can start anywhere in the alphabet and progress from there). For example, 'Andy's beautiful cat didn't ever fear getting hurt in jousting.'

Story games

- Tell a story orally by taking it in turns to add a sentence each until the story is complete.
- Make cards with names of characters (ghost, old man, postman, Henry VIII), settings (castle, desert island), objects (key, glass bottle), etc., and then pick one of each to create a story with.
- Keep a word journal, collecting new words and difficult spellings.
- Act out or rewrite well-known stories from a different point of view. For example, *Goldilocks* told from the point of view of Mummy Bear, *Peter Pan* from the point of view of Captain Hook, etc.

Choosing a task

Skill definition: Choosing which writing task to complete from a given list.

Different exams test your writing in different ways: some simply ask you to continue the text given for a comprehension exercise; others ask you to create a completely new piece of writing. You are often given a choice of topics and styles to choose from, although this is not always the case. Papers vary from year to year, so even if you have seen exam papers with no choice of writing task, read through this chapter to prepare yourself for the different styles of test.

Everyone has a form of writing they like best. You might like to write action-packed stories or descriptions of people and places. More mathematically minded people tend to enjoy writing factual pieces, which require logical thought rather than imagination. However, do not go into an exam room thinking, 'I am going to opt for the story, and not even think about anything else.' It might be that the story option leaves you cold, with no ideas whatsoever. If you were hoping to write a description, but there isn't one on the paper, then you will have to do something else. Let's have a look at how to make the best choice from whatever is in front of you.

Choose one of the following to write about:

1 Water
2 A persuasive article for the school magazine to campaign for the inclusion of an extra subject into the curriculum. You should:
   • explain what the subject is
   • give reasons why you think it should be included
   • suggest what should be removed from the curriculum to make way for it.
3 The playground at night
4 A time when you felt very proud of yourself

It is very easy, especially when in an exam room, to have a quick look at the questions and pick the first one you can do. Many people only ever pick the short titles, and don't even bother to read the long ones, such as number 2. You should give yourself the best chance, however, by thinking carefully about each option.

1 Water

This title is open to all sorts of writing. It could be:

● a narrative piece telling of a flood, perhaps, or a drought, when all that is on everyone's mind is water
● a descriptive piece, perhaps of a sea or river
● a **persuasive** piece looking at how important water is to life and how we need to work hard to conserve it.

Consider all of the possibilities before you start to plan. You may come up with alternative ideas of your own, but remember that the idea of 'water' needs to come through clearly.

2 A persuasive article for the school magazine

Unlike the previous title, which is left open to interpretation, you have to do what it says here. It is a good choice for those of you who do not particularly enjoy stories or description; it is much more factual and requires logic rather than imagination. It has the added bonus of already having been planned for you!

3 The playground at night

You would probably opt for a piece of description here. However, should you decide to use it as the setting for a story, do be careful not to let the story take over and lose the idea of 'the playground at night', for example by just starting in the playground and then moving away. It needs to be obvious to the reader why the story is called 'The playground at night'.

4 A time when you felt very proud of yourself

This title requires a personal response. It talks about 'you', so needs to be a true account – or at least one that could have happened to you (if you take something that happened to a friend and pretend it happened to you, no one will check!)

Whichever option you choose, be sure to think about all of the possibilities for each question before you start to write.

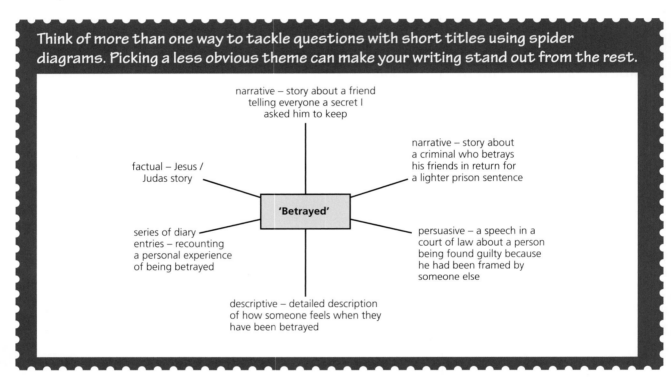

Think of more than one way to tackle questions with short titles using spider diagrams. Picking a less obvious theme can make your writing stand out from the rest.

narrative – story about a friend telling everyone a secret I asked him to keep

narrative – story about a criminal who betrays his friends in return for a lighter prison sentence

factual – Jesus / Judas story

'Betrayed'

series of diary entries – recounting a personal experience of being betrayed

persuasive – a speech in a court of law about a person being found guilty because he had been framed by someone else

descriptive – detailed description of how someone feels when they have been betrayed

Train

1   Look at the titles below, and think of as many different ways of interpreting the title as possible. Think about which text type you would use, the purpose of the piece and the vocabulary required. Use spider diagrams to list all of your ideas for each question.

   (a) The Supermarket

   (b) Friendship

   (c) Write about a time when you were treated unfairly.

Planning

Skill definition: Planning a range of different types of writing under ti

Before you start a writing task of any kind, you should always plan it fi
is to ensure you have a clear idea of what you are going to write and
writing to have direction, to avoid it being repetitive and to ensure it has
or purpose, depending on the type of writing you are doing.

There is no 'right' way to plan a piece of writing. As you write more, you will develop your o
preferred ways of planning but below are some ideas to get you started.

Remember, the plan should be short and succinct. It is a map of ideas for your writing and should
only consist of short notes or bullet points. It should be long enough to jog your memory and
outline your ideas but it is not a draft of the actual writing. There won't be enough time in an
exam to plan in fine detail.

Planning fiction

When planning a story, the key is to make sure it has a clear beginning, middle and end. You
wouldn't leave on a journey without knowing where you wanted to end up, and the same is true
of story writing.

Below are some ideas for how to write a plan:

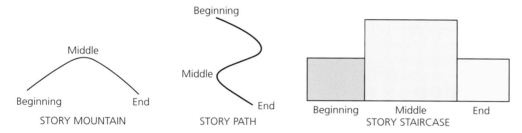

Annotate any of these shapes with quick notes about what will happen at each point of your
story. Don't use full sentences – there isn't time. Make sure the plot is logical and each part links
to the next.

- Beginning – set the scene, introduce the characters and set up the main problem/dilemma
- Middle – main action happens
- End – problem/dilemma is resolved satisfactorily (not with 'it was all a dream')

> In an exam, you probably won't have long to write so get into the action fairly quickly.
> It's not a novel – you don't have chapters to introduce the story. Make sure something
> happens quickly to keep the reader's attention.

You may prefer a simpler plan that maps out what you will include in each paragraph. This method
works for a wide range of writing types. For this example, imagine a fiction title of 'The Storm'.

P1 – Boy sitting in house in storm. Hears noises outside like a dog.

P2 – Goes outside and follows the sound. Dog trapped in deep muddy water. Boy tries to help but
also gets stuck.

P3 – Water rising. Both at risk. Father comes to rescue and they keep the stray dog as a pet.

...ng your plan, there are a number of things to think about to make your writing

...w to interpret the title

...en you look at the title, an obvious plot might jump out at you. Try to think beyond it and see ...w else you could interpret the title. Does the question have any words with a double meaning? ...Could you develop a metaphorical version of the title?

For example, **The Mirror** – this could be a fairy tale similar to Snow White but it could also be about identical twins, or about reflecting on yourself and your choices and decisions.

2 When and where to set the story

In many tasks, you have free choice about when and where to set your story. Make sure the title doesn't require a particular setting but otherwise you are free to choose. Consider different periods in history, different geographical locations, etc. Use the title to guide you.

For example, **Set in Stone** – this could be set in the Stone Age, or at Stonehenge or on Easter Island.

3 Which perspective to write from

If you really want your writing to stand out, try writing from an unusual perspective. Most stories are written in the third person from the perspective of a narrator. Try writing in role as one of the characters (first person) or not from a human point of view at all.

For example, **The Chase** – write as a deer being chased by a lion or from the point of view of a thief being pursued by the police.

Planning a description

You may choose a descriptive piece of writing for your fiction task. You still need to plan but in this case it will not have a beginning, middle and end like a story. Instead you should plan the different elements of the place or thing you are describing. Below are some ideas for structuring your writing:

- By sense, e.g. a paragraph each about what can be seen, heard, smelled, etc.
- As a tour, e.g. if describing a park, you might start with the trees, then the ponds, then the sky, then the flowers.
- By characteristic (for a character), e.g. if describing a villain, write a paragraph about his physical appearance, one about his walk and voice, another about his feelings and attitudes.
- By emotion, e.g. if describing a place you have visited, start by describing what made you happy, then what made you confused, what stuck in your memory, etc.

Planning non-fiction

When planning a non-fiction task, it is important to think of a number of valid and interesting points to make, whether it is for instruction, explanation, discussion or persuasion. Your plan enables you to group similar ideas together, to order your ideas and to write an effective introduction and conclusion.

You might use a mind map to gather ideas but it is useful to plan each paragraph to make sure you know which order you will write your points in.

Consider the task, 'Write a letter to your head teacher requesting that sport be made optional at school.'

Your plan might look something like:

Intro – Sport is not examined and so it is possible to get rid. Make children happier and give them ownership.

P1 – Embarrassment of not getting picked or not being good.

P2 – Plenty of opportunities in clubs or out of school.

P3 – Able to focus on academic subjects which will be examined.

Conclusion – Not asking to get rid of it entirely, just to offer choice. Children will be more engaged in lessons if they choose to be there.

The most important thing in any plan is that you use it while writing and refer back to it. It may change or develop slightly as you go along but you should follow it as closely as possible.

Although your plan will only be short, you may choose to add some vocabulary or imagery phrases into it if they come to mind.

Train

1 Home

Write a plan for this title but make sure the final text is not in the first person. You might also choose not to set it in the twenty-first century.

2 Winning

Write a plan for this title. The final text should be in the first person but make it clear that the person you are writing about is not you – pretend to be someone else.

3 The Kindness of Strangers

Write a plan for this title. Make sure the final text is not in the first person and is set in another time.

Test

Test time: 30:00

4 Choose your favourite plan and write it out in full. (25)

Narrative writing from a title

Skill definition: Creating a narrative based on a given title.

Questions which give you the title for a piece of writing require you to think of engaging and original ideas for a narrative which are **clearly** and **consistently** linked to the title.

Write a story entitled 'The Rescue'.

With a short title like this, you can interpret it almost any way you like. It could be a true story about something that happened to you. You could base it on a rescue you have read about in history. You could move away from the obvious idea of being rescued from some sort of physical danger and think about being rescued from a boring, humdrum life. The possibilities are endless!

In terms of structure, your short story should look like this:

In this way, most of your writing is devoted to the most important part of your story. It avoids writing too much description at the beginning and then running out of time for the exciting part of the piece. It is important to plan a clear ending so that the story is resolved satisfactorily.

When writing from a short title, you will do well to think beyond the obvious. Consider a range of ideas and think about different ways of reading the title.

Think about the 5 Ws: who, when, where, what, why.

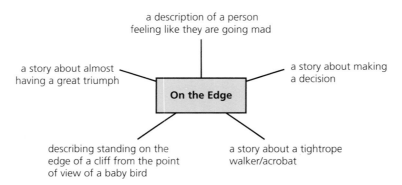

Here you could consider **why** a character is on the edge, **who** is on the edge, **where** the edge is, **what** kind of edge is it and, **when** they are no longer on the edge whether that is a relief or a tragedy.

Make sure you consider different perspectives and text types. Your story might start at the end and work its way back to the beginning using a flashback.

> It is really important that your story idea is closely related to the title all the way through. It must not seem as if you have just written a story of your choice and briefly mentioned the title for the sake of it.

Train

1   Plan a story for each of the following story titles:
   (a) Courage **(b)** The Longest Journey **(c)** The Alarm **(d)** What Might Have Been **(e)** Ghosts

Responding to textual prompts

Skill definition: Writing from a longer written prompt.

Including a given phrase or sentence in a composition

Questions that give a piece of text as the starting point generally take one of two forms. You may be given the opening or closing sentence of a story. You may be given a short statement or quotation that allows you to develop a story in a number of directions.

> Write a story that contains the line: 'I knew as soon as I looked at him that something was wrong.'

Look carefully at the question before you begin your plan:

- You are not told where the line has to come, so it can be at the beginning, in the middle or at the end of your story.
- You are told to write a **story**, so make sure that it has a clear beginning, middle and end.
- Your story should be in the **first person**, as this is how the line is written.

It is important not to change the words if you are given a line of text to include, so make sure that you copy them down carefully.

Now, look carefully at these examples to see how you are guided on what you need to write.

> 'Despite the silence, he knew that there was someone there.'

Whether or not you are told to put this at the beginning or the end, you *must* write in the **third person** ('**he** knew that there was someone there'). Who 'he' is, or where 'he' is, is entirely up to you, however.

> 'The dark, forbidding land stretched far away.'

In this example you can write in either the first person or the third person. The 'dark, forbidding land' can be anywhere you like: in this world or even on another planet.

Train ●

1 Plan a story that includes the following line at the beginning or end: 'Suddenly, it vanished.'

Using a quote as a starting point

Sometimes, you are given a well-known saying or a proverb as your title. Examples include:

- Cheats never prosper.
- Practice makes perfect.
- More haste, less speed.
- Never judge a book by its cover.

Before planning your writing, think about the meaning of the phrase and how you are going to build it into your piece.

- It may serve as a moral for your story.
- It may be interpreted literally.
- You could use it as a first or last line.
- It could be said by a character in your story.

As with all tasks, you must make sure that the quote is the cornerstone of your story. It cannot just be bolted on to the end if it doesn't relate to the whole of the rest of the story.

Try to be original: some proverbs relate to common fables or fairy tales but if you can move away from this, your story will stand out more.

For example: never judge a book by its cover – this might suggest a **Beauty and the Beast** type story but there are many other options:

- You could take this metaphorical saying literally, e.g. write about a book that turns out to have something hidden in it.
- You could write about an unlikely friendship, between people or between animals that wouldn't normally get on together, e.g. a chicken and a fox.
- You might choose to combine the idea of books with the metaphorical meaning of the proverb and write as a librarian with a secret second life.
- You might write as a book on the shelf in the library that never gets chosen due to its old-fashioned cover.

> If you don't know what the proverb or saying means, then it is advisable not to choose this task if you have the choice. You could set yourself up for a fall.

Train

2 'You win some, you lose some.' Plan a composition based on this saying.

> Always read the instructions carefully. You may be given a sentence to include somewhere or it might have to be the last line of the story. Copy it word for word when you use it and make sure you put it in the right place.

Train

3 Write a plan for the following tasks:

  (a) Write a story beginning in the following way: 'It came out of nowhere.'

  (b) Write a story with the title 'The Lost Letter'.

  (c) Courage. Write about this in any way you choose.

Test

Test time: 30:00

4 Choose one of the following tasks to plan and write.   (25)

  (a) Lost and Found. Write a story with this title.

  (b) Write a story that begins or ends with the sentence, 'I couldn't believe my eyes.'

  (c) Write in a style of your choice including the sentence, 'Finally, he understood what he needed to do.'

Responding to pictures

Skill definition: Planning a piece of writing based on a picture.

When faced with a picture to write about, do not think that the only thing you can do is to describe what you see. You can also use your imagination to 'get into' the picture and use it as the starting point for a story or other text type. The examiner will be looking for an original and imaginative response which clearly relates to the picture but which looks at it in an unusual and thoughtful way.

Example exam question

Use this picture as a starting point for a piece of writing.

The key to interpreting the picture well is considering all the elements of it. Use the 5 Ws to help you: **where** is the picture, **who** might be there, **what** does it sound like, **why** does it look the way it does, **when** will you describe it (morning, noon, night)?

Also think about what you associate with what is in the picture. In this case:

- Is it a rainforest? An enchanted forest?
- Who lives there and how could they feature in a story: tribespeople, animals, hunters?
- Which wider issues are associated with this picture: deforestation, animal conservation etc.?
- Can you use ideas from books you have read that have similar settings or themes?

Writing about people

A picture like this gives you lots of options.

1 First consider text type: narrative or description? This will depend on the picture. If there is action in the picture then a story might work best. If it just a scene then a description might work better.

2   Identify a particular point of interest: is there one face with a particular expression or one group of people that stands out? Can you spot any clear relationships between any two people? Does someone look suspicious?

3   Use the context of the picture to help you decide when and where the story will be set. Is it modern or old? Is it in this country or another? Look for details that will help guide your story planning.

Writing about places and events

You could be faced with two types of landscape: one without anything happening such as the picture on page 95, or a scene with an event as on this page. In either case, you should aim to come up with an original and engaging idea. This is particularly important with something like the tennis match as just writing about a tennis match is rather obvious and won't stand out.

Consider the following:

1   Could you write from a different perspective? Write as the loser of the match, looking back at the game. Write as the tennis ball but don't give away that's what you are until near the end.

2   Create a story using the events in the picture. Could the match have been delayed due to something?

3   Make sure you use plenty of description, even if it seems like a fairly mundane, everyday scene. Show off your skills to the best of your ability.

> Make brief annotations on the picture if you are able to, highlighting important or interesting features.

Train

1   Write two different plans for pieces of writing that use the picture of the forest as a starting point.

2   Write two different plans for pieces of writing that use the 'writing about people' picture as a starting point. One of them must be told in the first person.

3   Write two plans for pieces of writing that use the 'writing about places and events' picture as a starting point. One must be fiction and one must be non-fiction.

Test

Test time: 30:00

4   Choose one of the plans you have prepared and write it up in full.   (25)

Continuation

Skill definition: Continuing a story that you have read, incorporating its stylistic and plot features.

Often in an exam you will be asked to continue the extract that you read in the comprehension part of the exam. This is sometimes the only composition task, it may be the last question in the comprehension (and worth a considerable number of marks) or it could be a separate composition task. It is a popular task for examiners to set because you need to show writing skills as well as accurate understanding of the text.

Third person, past tense | *One main character, Max* | *Something unsettling has happened* | *Lots of questions*

As he climbed into bed, Max thought about the day's events. He was still confused. What had really happened? Did he really see his father's face at the window? But that was impossible: his father was on the other side of the world. His mother was adamant that he would never see his father again. But he was there, wasn't he?

Max pulled the cosy duvet right up to his shoulders and tucked his feet under the end. Warm and safe. He always felt warm and safe in his bed. He quickly drifted off to sleep and soon the dreams came again…

Key hint that the next part of the story should be about the dream | *Key detail about the other character* | *This is a recurring dream and possibly not a happy one* | *Foreshadowing that perhaps he won't be safe this time*

Question: Continue the extract you have read, writing the next three paragraphs of the story. Use the style of the original author.

There are a number of things to consider when approaching a question like this.

- Reread the extract and think about what logically could happen next.
- Consider the characters and what you already know about them. Their actions and words must match the kind of person they are.
- Think about the setting. Your writing must echo the historical era, geographical setting, etc.
- Look at the style of the author. Do they use lots of dialogue? Are there many poetic devices? Do they write many long sentences or a string of shorter ones?

You can find out more about how to continue their style effectively on pages 112–113.

As with all tasks, you should plan this out before you start writing. There are some key things to remember:

- Make sure your story is in the same tense and person as the original. Most stories are in the past tense and third person but always check!
- Do not be overambitious about how far ahead in the story you can go in the time you have been given. For example, if the original story lasted a few hours then your continuation might include the next hour or two, not the next three weeks!
- Make references back to events, characters, etc., from the original to show you are clearly continuing it rather than writing a new story entirely.

- Ensure that you follow on from exactly where the story finished.
- Don't include anything that contradicts what has already happened. For example, a grumpy, miserable character cannot suddenly become generous and cheerful for no reason.

Train

As they finally made it to the top of the misty hill, their aching legs gave out on them. Thomas turned to his companion. "We made it!" he whispered. Then louder, "We finally made it!"
A feeling of great relief washed over them both and they smiled despite the pain and uncertainty they had already encountered. They were safe.
"Over there," uttered William nervously. "What's that? No … no. It can't be!"

1   Consider the extract above. Make some bullet points to answer the following questions.

   (a) What do you know about the characters?

   (b) What do you know about the setting?

   (c) Which style features could you copy?

   (d) What clues are there about what could happen next?

2   Plan a continuation of the story.

Test

Test time: 30:00

3   Read the text below and continue the story. Aim to write 3–4 paragraphs.   (25)

   As the door clicked shut, I was alone. Hidden. Safe. For now … I had escaped temporarily but it wouldn't be long until the spell wore off. The wizards weren't stupid and it wouldn't be long before they noticed that they had been tricked. If I were to survive, I had to escape the castle before they noticed the book was missing. I looked around me, wracking my brains for a plan.

Book review

Skill definition: Planning a book review that avoids re-telling the story.

The most common mistake that people make when writing book reviews is to spend most of their time re-telling the story, rather than actually reviewing it. This is not the purpose of a book review and should be avoided.

Focus instead on the good and bad elements of the books – the characters, descriptions, language, tension, etc. You should also include your own response to the book. Did it make you laugh? Were you unable to put it down? Was it full of cliffhangers?

1   Write about a book that was very memorable, explaining why you remember it so well.

In this question, the focus is on what it is *you* like about the book you have chosen to write about and why you enjoyed it so much. Try to include at least one sentence that describes how you reacted to the book in every paragraph you write.

All book reviews should look at two main aspects of a book – the characters and the plot – so this is the place to begin when planning.

When planning your book review, think paragraph by paragraph and use the chronology of the book to help you. For example:

● Introduction – general theme/topic of the book and brief opinion overall
● P1 – quick rundown of the plot without giving too much away
● P2 – analysis of two key characters
● P3 – your opinion with reasons and evidence
● Conclusion – overall opinion, recommendation, etc.

Throughout the composition, remember to use language relevant to books such as 'a real page-turner', 'unputdownable', 'a thrilling read', etc. Refer to specific elements of a book. The vocabulary below will help you:

plot	plot twist	flashback	characterisation	suspense	cliffhanger	setting
humour	mystery	horror	adventure	science fiction	moral/message	
theme	symbolism	historical context	ending			

Characters
● Choose your favourite one or two characters and think about what it is you like about them. Are they funny, for example, or brave, or really horrible?
● Note down the aspects of their character that illustrate what you like about them.
● Note down examples that you can use in your review. When you come to write your review, describe the example briefly.

For example:

I admired Wes for the way in which he stood up to Piggy Bacon and would not let his spirit be crushed by him. Even when he was punished for telling Piggy he was wrong, he stood up proudly to him and did not give up. I was really happy when he escaped and nearly cheered when I realised what he had done.

The plot

When thinking about the plot, note down:

● who told the story (was it one of the characters or a narrator – or was it told by more than one character?)
● what for you were the most memorable parts of the book (think about why you remember them and how you reacted to them)
● any parts that surprised you – or that you had predicted would happen.

For example:

> After the Aborigines found Arthur and Marty in the outback, I had no idea what was going to happen to them. When they were taken to Meg's, I was really glad that they had found someone to take care of them at last. The part when they lived with her was completely different from everything that had come before, and everything that happened afterwards. This is a book of many parts.

Other things to comment on:

● Setting – Did you learn anything about the place or time the book was set in?
● Structure – Did the book have an unusual structure or was it told from a different viewpoint? How did this add to your enjoyment of the book?

Personal response

Finally, all book reviews should include a detailed description of your response as you read it. Perhaps you defied your parents and did not turn out your light at a certain time because you did not want to stop reading; perhaps it made you laugh out loud, or cry; or perhaps you disliked it so much you had to drag yourself through it chapter by painful chapter. Use expressions such as:

● I couldn't stop laughing when …
● I just couldn't bear it when …
● When I closed the book at the end I felt …

Train

1 Write a plan for each of the following questions:

(a) Write about a book that made you laugh, explaining why it was so humorous.

(b) Write a review of the most memorable book you have read.

(c) Write a review of a book you have studied at school.

> It can be very frustrating to start writing a book review, only to forget the names of some of the characters or places. Draw up a list of your three favourite books from the last year and make brief notes on the names of the characters, what happens, where the book is set and how you reacted to it when you read it for the first time. Keep the notes and look over them just before your exam so that you can bring the relevant information to mind.

Test

Test time: 30:00

2 Write about a book you did not enjoy. (25)

Personal response

Skill definition: Planning a piece of writing that requires a personal response.

A personal response needs to include plenty of detail about how you reacted to something that happened to you; there should therefore be lots of description of your thoughts and feelings.

As you will be writing about something that has happened to you, do *not* make it up. It will sound unbelievable. It is, however, fine to exaggerate or embellish the details to make your writing more exciting or interesting. You could write the piece in the form of a true story or a diary.

One of the benefits of writing a personal response is that you do not have to invent characters or settings; you already know what happened as you were there! However, you must re-create the event clearly and vividly so that the reader can picture the whole scene and share your thoughts and feelings about what happened.

There are certain things to be wary of when writing personal responses:

● You will be writing in the first person but don't repeatedly start sentences with 'I'.
● Make sure you convey the detail on the page: you were there when it happened but your reader was not.
● If the events happened when you were very young, make sure you describe them using mature and sophisticated language: you don't want to sound like the age you were.
● Keep to the interesting bits of the story and avoid unnecessary waffle.
● Don't get too personal: include emotions and feelings but don't go overboard.
● Use synonyms to avoid repeating the key word from the question.

Think of your writing as a kind of story: this will ensure you use all the exciting story-telling techniques you know and it will make your personal recount more engaging for the reader.

Use of figurative language
Short sentences to start and add impact
Use of ellipses to build tension
Don't reveal the source of the fear too quickly

> Quivering. Shaking. I couldn't stop. I couldn't control myself. The hairs on the back of my neck pricked up like cactus needles. Beads of sweat began to form on my forehead. My knees felt like jelly. My biggest fear… Right ahead of me… The sea!
>
> To a child of three, the sea was an endless expanse of watery danger. As the waves rose and fell, I watched mesmerised. Staying at a safe distance, I could only imagine the horrors that lurked beneath; sharks, sea snakes, piranhas, four-headed blood-sucking mutant fish. My imagination began to run away with me when I heard the dreaded words, 'Let's go paddle!'

Show a childlike worry using grown-up language
Use of dialogue to add interest

Write about a time when you were frightened.

Look at the example question above. The key word here is **frightened**. The fact that you were frightened should come through strongly, and not get lost in descriptions of other things.

You could approach the story in a number of ways but two ideas are outlined below:

- Narrative recounting the events in the form of a story. This will be in the first person (I, me, etc.)
- A diary entry explaining the day's events as if you were reflecting back on them at the end of the day. You already know what has happened so bear that in mind when you are writing.

Both versions should include description and emotion and refer back to the key word 'frightened'.

Train

1 Imagine you were given the following questions. Identify the key word that you will need to focus on in each question.

   (a) Write about a time when you needed to be brave.

   (b) Describe the most memorable day of your life.

   (c) Write about the most spectacular place you have ever visited.

   (d) Write about a challenge you have faced.

   (e) Describe a time when you felt disappointed.

2 Write a plan for a page from a diary for each of the questions above.

3 Rewrite your plans on the same topics, but this time in the form of a true story.

> When practising writing about a topic, use a highlighter pen to highlight all the bits in your writing that relate to the title. If the highlighting makes up less than half of what you have written, go back and write some more!

Test

Test time: 30:00

4 Write about a time when you were frightened.   (25)

Discursive and persuasive writing

Skill definition: Understanding the similarities and differences between persuasive and discursive writing.

Both discursive and persuasive writing need to include facts and opinions.

● Discursive writing puts forward *both* sides of an argument, after which the writer reaches a conclusion.
● Persuasive writing puts *one* side of an argument and, as its name suggests, tries to persuade the reader to agree with the writer.

When planning your writing, you should follow each point you make with an example to illustrate that point (this applies both to discursive and persuasive texts). You will also need a short introduction and a short conclusion of a few sentences each.

Write an article for a school magazine in which you look at the advantages and disadvantages of wearing school uniform.

Firstly, think about the audience you are writing for. This is a school magazine, so it will be read by other children, parents and teachers. Make sure there is something of interest to each of these groups.

Discursive texts

The title above suggests this will be a discursive text since you are asked to put both sides of the argument – for and against wearing uniform. Begin planning with a list of advantages and disadvantages related to the topic.

Plan out each paragraph, grouping ideas together. Make sure you include an introduction and conclusion. For example:

Paragraph 1: Introduce the topic and explain that there are a range of arguments on each side.

Paragraph 2: Outline the advantages with examples.

Paragraph 3: Outline the disadvantages with examples.

Paragraph 4: Conclude the article, summarising what you have written about.

Persuasive texts

Persuasive writing is very similar to discursive writing, but it does not consider all of the arguments – it looks at only one side. So, if you were asked to write a persuasive text on the benefits of school uniform, you would use only half of the arguments on the plan above. However, you should remember to illustrate every point you make with an example and, as you have fewer points to make, you can use more than one example for each point. This type of text is often seen in the form of a letter.

Several techniques can be used in persuasive writing to make it more convincing:

● Rhetorical questions

Wouldn't it be better if we could choose what to wear?

● Persuasive sentence openers that make your ideas sound more believable

- It is clear that …
- Obviously …
- Everybody agrees that …
- Research shows …
- Evidence proves that …

- Confident verbs to make you sound credible

I believe   I know   I am sure   I am certain

Speech writing

A speech is another form of persuasive text, but you need to plan it slightly differently from a written article because the audience has to remember what you say – they cannot refer back to what you said earlier. Because of that, you have to use some repetition, especially of the most important points. Your plan should be in the following form:

- Tell the audience briefly what you are going to say, for example:

Today I am going to consider all of the advantages of living in the countryside. I will be explaining the benefits to your health and describing the pleasures of being close to nature.

- Make all of your points, with an example to illustrate each one. These might include: the health benefits of a lack of pollution, fresh food and the less stressful pace of life; you could then describe the beauty of the scenery, seeing first-hand where your food comes from, being more aware of the change in seasons, etc. Each new point should be in a new paragraph.
- Summary. Unlike a piece of writing, you then briefly summarise what you have said.

In short, tell your audience what you are going to say, say it, then tell them what you said!

> If you are asked to write a letter, you must set it out correctly including your address, Dear, the date and an appropriate sign-off: 'yours sincerely' if you addressed the person by name, 'yours faithfully' if you addressed it to Sir or Madam or their position (e.g. Prime Minister).

Train

1   Decide whether the following tasks are persuasive or discursive:

   (a) Write a balanced argument based on the following statement – 'Everybody should have a pet.'

   (b) Write a letter to your local MP asking them to consider taking action to reduce traffic in your local area.

   (c) Write a speech for a debate about people wearing real fur. You may choose which side of the argument to argue for.

   (d) Write a website article about the importance and dangers of social media.

   (e) Imagine you are running for Prime Minister. Write a speech to your voters, convincing them to vote for you.

2   Plan an article for a school magazine in which you try to persuade pupils and staff that getting rid of school uniform would be a very good thing.

3   Plan a speech in which you try to convince your classmates that it is better to live in the countryside than in a town.

4   Plan a persuasive letter to your head teacher in which you argue either for or against changing the school into a single-sex or mixed school, depending on what it is already.

Test

Test time: 30:00

5   Write a speech arguing either for or against children being given the vote.   (25)

Starting and ending your writing

Skill definition: Using exciting story starters to engage the reader and ending compositions effectively.

Making and leaving an impression

When you are planning your writing, it is important to begin thinking about interesting ways you can start and end your work.

- You should be trying to set the mood or the tone of the writing straight away and maintain it right until the end. In an exam, your piece of writing will only be short so every words counts.
- The beginning and the end of a composition are often what the reader remembers the most so make sure they have a strong impact.

Starting your writing

Your opening needs to grab the reader's attention and make him or her want to read on. This is called a hook. Remember that the first sentence of your composition is the first impression an examiner will have of your writing so it is worth making it the very best that you can. Here are some ways to open stories that you might like to try.

Open with dialogue

"I don't think I can stand this much longer," Peter groaned.

This makes the reader start thinking: 'Can't stand what?', 'Who is Peter?' and they read on to find answers to their questions.

Open with description

I looked up and didn't like what I saw. Huge, grey clouds filled the sky and a biting wind had blown up, causing me to shiver with both cold and fear.

The reader will wonder why you are so worried about the clouds as you have dropped a hint about what might happen next. They will want to read on to find out if they are correct.

Open with action

As the wave hit the boat, I shot through the air and hit the icy water. The shock knocked the air out of my lungs and I struggled to get back to the surface.

This is dramatic and exciting and suggests to the reader that the whole story will be full of action and thrills.

Open with a question

Have you ever seen your life flash before your eyes? I have.

Open with a single word sentence (or series of them)

Thunder. A single crack of thunder. I looked up to the cloudless sky and wondered how a beautiful blue panorama could yield such a terrifying sound.

This can build tension and mystery as you slowly reveal what is going on.

Ending your writing

When you plan a composition, having a good ending is vital. It is the last thing the examiner reads and it must resolve or sum everything up satisfactorily. It should feel like it was planned and that you did not just stop writing.

Whether it is a story, a letter or a speech, the ending is vital to make sure the reader feels that they have read an entire piece and that they are left with something memorable.

Ending stories:

- A happy ending where the dilemma or the problem of the story is solved and explained to the reader. For example:

As the smoke subsided, Amar could see his father in the distance, safe, unharmed and walking towards him with open arms.

- A return to where the story started. For example:

Luke had won. The medal was his, just as he had imagined all those weeks ago.

- A cliffhanger where something remains mysterious or intriguing to the reader. This has to be carefully planned and should make sense in the context of the story. For example:

They all breathed a sigh of relief as the helicopter soared up into the sky. The threat had been removed. For now …

- The main character reflects on what has happened or what he or she has learned from the experience. For example:

As the sun set on the most frightening week of his life, Jamal finally felt like the brave young soldier he had always known he could be.

Don't overdo the ending or write far beyond the point when the story has been resolved. This is unnecessary and detracts from a good ending.

Ending non-fiction writing:

- Rhetorical questions

Sharks: evil killers or elegant kings of the ocean?

- Food for thought

Children are the leaders of the future: give them the education they deserve.

- Statement of belief

To conclude, all of the evidence points to the environment being the only global issue worth spending our tax money on.

Train

1 Write a plan for a story called 'The Other Side'.

2 Write three possible opening sentences for your story – use different techniques chosen from the suggestions above.

3 Write a plan for a non-fiction piece with the title 'Our World'.

4 Write three possible closing sentences for your writing.

5 Write either of the compositions you have planned.

Test

Test time: 30:00

6 Write a story called 'In the Dark'.

(25)

Improving your writing: adverbials

Skill definition: Using adverbials to add detail to writing.

Adding detail to your writing will gain you more marks for style and vocabulary. All writing needs detail in one form or another. This might be description, explanation, examples, etc. Adverbial phrases will help you to add this.

Adverbial phrases are similar to adverbs. They describe an action using a short phrase and tell you:

- **how** something happened
- **when** it happened
- **where** it happened
- **how** often it happened.

Here are some examples:

- How – She ran to the shops *as fast as her legs could carry her*.
- When – *In the middle of the night*, she heard a knock at the door.
- Where – The flag *on the top of the building* swayed in the wind.
- How often – *Every weekend*, we visit a different museum.

If the adverbial contains a verb, it is called an **adverbial clause**. For example:

She opened the fridge, *looking for a snack*.

After he opened the safe, he looked around furtively.

Standing on top of the hill, he screamed at the top of his lungs.

Notice how they can be placed in different parts of a sentence, either before or after the verb.

> When an adverbial is placed at the start of a sentence, it should be followed with a comma.

Train

1 Add an adverbial phrase or clause to these sentences. Note down whether it tells you how, when, where or how often.

(a) She opened the front door.

(b) They watched the fireworks.

(c) The sprinter reached the finish line.

(d) Everybody opened their presents.

2 Use these adverbials in a full sentence.

(a) as the clock struck two

(b) with a smile on his face

(c) under the bridge

(d) every other day

Test

Test time: 30:00

3 Write a story with the opening words 'As the clock struck two …'. Aim to use at least ten adverbials in your story. Highlight them when you have finished. (25)

Improving your writing: flashbacks

Skill definition: Using flashbacks effectively in a short story.

A good way to show maturity in your writing is to include a brief flashback. It shows awareness of different ways to write narrative, an ability to manipulate tenses accurately and adds interest and texture to your writing.

A flashback is when a story jumps back in time, usually to explain something that is happening now or to give detail about a memory a character has. It should only be used if it adds to or furthers the plot of your story or gives necessary background information about your character.

When you write a flashback you need to consider the following points:

● How will you signal to the reader that you are jumping back in time?
● What is the purpose of the flashback? What background information does it give?
● How will you indicate that the flashback has finished?

Here is an example:

Signal that the flashback will start

As Julia was lying in bed, she couldn't stop thinking about what to do next. Her parents were furious; they wouldn't talk to her. Her best friend was missing. She thought back to that horrible night ...

Use of 'had' (pluperfect tense) to show that the action is further back in the past than the main story

Dark. It had been incredibly dark. Nothing could be seen or heard until she had noticed that faint whimpering sound. But what was it? She wished she had gone further into the woods, been braver but ...

Signal that the flashback has ended

Clue that adds to the plot

"Julia!" She was jolted back to reality. "Julia, quickly. Downstairs!" her mother shrieked. She launched herself off the bed and hurtled downstairs.

> At the end of a flashback, use an ellipsis (...) to show that a character's memory or thought was interrupted by something happening in the present.

Train

1 Continue these sentences, which could be used to start a flashback:

  (a) She thought harder ...

  (b) Suddenly she caught a glimpse in her mind of ...

  (c) He wondered ...

  (d) Paul couldn't stop thinking ...

2 Continue these sentences, which could be used to end a flashback:

  (a) Without warning ...

  (b) She was startled ...

  (c) The bell rang and ...

  (d) As the light flicked on ...

Test

Test time: 30:00

3 Write a story entitled 'Missing' and include a short flashback within it. (25)

Improving your writing: imagery and descriptive techniques

Skill definition: Using language to create interest and involve the reader.

Whatever type of writing you are doing, whether it is telling a story, describing a place or a person, or trying to persuade the reader about something, it is important to write in such a way that you put pictures (images) in the reader's head. In this way, your writing will not only be more interesting, it will be more memorable.

Think back to the chapter on comprehension (pages 73–75) and you may remember how effective figurative language can be. Be inspired by what you have read and include it in your own work.

Using some of the following 'writers' tricks' will help to 'lift' your writing and make it more interesting.

- **Using the senses**
  Without realising it, we use our senses all the time to build up a picture of someone or something. When you are writing description, don't just use the sense of sight – what about sounds and smells, for example? The more senses you use, the clearer the picture will be for the reader.

- **Alliteration**
  The repetition of a consonant at the beginning of a string of words adds a 'sound' quality to your writing. Use it in writing to add emphasis in non-fiction or to create a sound in the reader's head in fiction writing or to add to the mood of a description. For example:

  The slender stream snaked its way through the countryside.

- **Onomatopoeia**
  When the sound of the word is similar to the sound of what it describes, the technique is called onomatopoeia. Use it in your writing to help the reader hear your description. It works well when used during action-packed scenes, mysterious episodes or describing places where the sound adds to the mood.

  screech   crunch   sizzle   pop   jingle   gurgle   rattle   twang

- **Similes**
  A simile is used to compare two things to help the reader imagine them. By giving the reader more of a visual picture, the qualities of the thing being described are easier to comprehend. Use similes in descriptive writing to build a vivid picture. Use them in non-fiction writing to help the reader understand your viewpoint or to help convince them of something by deepening their understanding.

  The tallest trees towered over the rest of the forest like giants marching through clipped grass.

● Metaphors

Like similes, metaphors also compare two things but on a deeper level. Rather than describing one as thing as similar to another, metaphors describe something as if it were something else. This makes a description go far deeper and allows you to build a broader picture of what something is like.

As he travelled the road from adolescence to adulthood, he passed alongside many places to stop and many to keep walking past.

● Personification

Giving human attributes to things that are not human is called personification. It may be actions, emotions or abilities. Use it in horror or mystery to make things seem creepier or in adventure to emphasise the action. It can be used to add emotion to a story or to make something seem more powerful in a piece of persuasive writing.

As we walked through the wood, the trees on either side of the path leaned over to hear better what we were saying. The path narrowed as they put out their arms to join hands and prevent us from reaching our destination.

● Groups of three

The tricolon is a group of three words or phrases. It creates rhythm: use it to add emphasis and help an idea stick in the reader's mind. It can also be combined with alliteration. For example:

As I regained consciousness, I felt beaten, bruised and battered.

● Interesting verbs

Choose interesting verbs and don't repeat a verb in a piece of writing. Think about what action is happening and consider a range of synonyms. Which one fits the mood, the character or the setting the best? In this example, you could think about the speed of the boy, the way he moves and the tone of voice of the narrator:

He trudged/sprinted/plodded/dragged himself up the hill to school.

● Interesting adjectives

The same is true of adjectives. Don't just pick an interesting adjective – pick the most appropriate one. Sometimes one well-chosen word tells the reader all they need to know.

Beautiful? Or dazzling, ravishing, stunning?

Serious? Or severe, solemn, maudlin?

● Avoid 'dead' words and phrases such as 'there was/were/is/are'. Instead, replace these words with ones that are more descriptive and informative. For example, rather than saying 'There were lots of people in the room' try:

Hundreds of people were crammed into the room.

1 Improve these sentences using some of the techniques described above. You could change a word or rewrite the entire sentence. Try not to change the meaning.

(a) We heard a loud sound.

(b) Everybody went into the house.

(c) The buildings were tall and had glass windows.

(d) The sun shone on the water.

(e) We were afraid.

(f) She felt the sun on her face.

(g) The ship sailed across the ocean.

(h) The thunder crashed and the lightning flashed.

Test • • • • • • • • • • • • • • • • • • • Test time: 30:00

2 Write a description of the most beautiful place in the world. (25)

Improving your writing: mimicking style

Skill definition: Copying the style of an author when continuing a story.

As you saw on pages 97–98, the task of continuing the story used in the comprehension is a common task in 11+ exams. It is important when doing this that your style of writing echoes that of the original author. The continuation should be seamless and in order to do this you need to identify the styles and techniques the author used in the first place.

You should always reread the passage before starting and identify the following features:

● Which tense and person did the author write in?
● Did they use dialogue and how much?
● How much imagery and description did they use? What kind of imagery did they use?
● Did they use simple or complex sentences, or a mixture of the two?
● What was the pace of the story? Did it cover a long or short period of time?

All of these elements can and should be copied when you start your continuation.

Other things you need to mimic are:

● the number of characters and their traits – you won't have time to introduce lots more characters into the story
● the setting and its atmosphere – there isn't usually the time in a short continuation to depart from the given setting
● the genre – if the story is historical fiction, you need to incorporate the features of this genre in your continuation.

Look at this example:

Clue about the genre.
This is science fiction.

Description of the setting

Third person and past tense

As the moon came into view through the shuttle's control centre window, Irim knew that the adventure was only just beginning. He thought back to his life on Earth, his family anxiously waiting for news of his safe arrival on the Space Station, his comfortable bed and normal clothes. That was a world away now from the cramped quarters of the shuttle and
5   the cumbersome and bulky space suits. Speckled and magnificent, the silvery moon hung in the air like a glimmering bauble on a Christmas tree. He had never imagined he would see it from such a different viewpoint.

Use of imagery

Main characters

Suddenly, Vladimir, another member of the crew, radioed through a message. He reported, "Unusual activity observed, check the radar screens immediately."
10   "Message received," Irim replied as he manoeuvred himself towards the radar station. He looked at the screen and froze.

Use of dialogue

Clue about what will happen next. Something unexpected has been discovered.

The whole passage covers around five minutes of real time so your continuation should cover the next five minutes of the story.

All of these features of the text should be mimicked in a continuation. What actually happens next will be a product of your imagination, what you know about sciencefiction stories and the clues you have seen.

Train

Stars peppered the night like flecks of diamond. Gentle breezes ticked the leaves on the trees. The reflection of the golden moon, high in the sky, shimmered in the ripples on the lake. It was unusually beautiful for a spring night.

As Ben made his way down towards the water, he felt calm, peaceful and entirely alone. His midnight paddles were the only secret he had. Sneaking out of his bedroom window, without waking his mum, he felt free. What she didn't know wouldn't hurt her, would it? All of his worries melted away as his feet hit the cold water on the lake shore.

1   Identify key details about the setting to help you continue the story.
2   Find clues about the characters that will be important in your story continuation.
3   Make a list of some style features of the writing which you can use in your continuation.
4   Is there any foreshadowing or subtle hints at what might come next?

Test
Test time: 30:00

5   Continue the story above using the features identified. Aim to write the next three paragraphs.

(25)

Improving your writing: sentence structure

Skill definition: Using a range of sentence structures to add texture and rhythm to your writing.

Another way to add texture and interest to your work is to vary the way you have put your sentences together. Writing that contains only sentences of the same length and shape is flat and dull. By varying the length and shape of your sentences you can emphasise certain parts, add tension or change the pace of the piece of writing. Try these:

- Vary the **length** of your sentences. When describing someone or something, use longer sentences; short sentences are better for rapid action or for impact. When writing about the same thing, it is a good idea to make your sentences gradually shorter. Here is an example:

Instead of: I approached the house. I could hear voices coming from inside. There was a light coming through the curtains. They were not closed properly. I walked up the path to the door. I rang the bell. The voices stopped.

Try: Approaching the house I could hear voices from inside and saw a light through the partly closed curtains. I walked up the path to the door and rang the bell. Everything went quiet.

- Vary the **shape** of your sentences as well. If you are writing a story about someone called Henry, don't begin every sentence with 'Henry' or 'he'.

Instead of: Henry dragged himself to the Maths room and sat down. He did not like Maths. He hated it, in fact. He got out his books and looked round. He could not see the teacher. Good. He was glad. He hoped the teacher was away.

Try something like: Dragging himself to the Maths room, Henry sat down. He did not like Maths: hated it, in fact. Getting out his books, he looked around. No teacher. He smiled, hoping she was away.

- Vary the **way you start** your sentences. Here are some good ways to do this:
  - Use -ly words

Quickly, he ran to the door.

  - Use adverbial phrases

At the peak of the hill, he yelled for help.

  - Use -ing words

Shivering, she warmed herself by the fire.

  - Use -ed words

Exhausted, he collapsed in the chair.

  - Use prepositions

Down the hill, he made his descent.

- Use conjunctions

However, he couldn't find the key.

● Vary the **type of writing** you use. Some of your story might be dialogue but it must be balanced with narration. Using too much conversation is confusing and hard to follow. It should be used to add to the story rather than for its own sake.

Look at these pieces of writing. The writer took the original piece then used some 'writers' tricks' to improve it.

Version 1

I entered the forest. I looked around to see what was there. I squinted to see as it was dark. There were lots of trees. I could not turn back because I had a mission to do.

The shadows were dark and frightening. The trees seemed to be watching me. I wanted to go home but I could not go back because of my mission.

Version 2

Simple sentences have been joined to make compound and complex sentences, and repetition of the word 'I' has been avoided.

I entered the forest and looked around. As my eyes adjusted to the gloom, I saw the trees watching over me. But I could not turn back – I was on a mission.

The shadows hid deep, dark secrets and flitted from tree to tree. The spies of the forest were doing their job, watching my every move. All I wanted to do was turn back to the warmth and safety of my home. But I could not turn back – I was on a mission.

Movement has been added together with personification. There is more description about how comforting their home is in comparison with the forest.

Train

1 Improve this piece of writing.

I turned on my torch but it did not make it much easier to see. I carried on as best I could. The trees made it difficult to move and I kept bashing into branches and leaves. But I could not go back – I had to keep going on.

After a long time I realised I was on a path. I had reached the road and was finally out of the wood! I had not turned back. I had completed my mission.

2 Take one of the timed pieces of work you have already written and improve it using some of the suggestions here.

Test

Test time: 30:00

3 Write a description of one of the following: (25)

(a) The Woodland

(b) A Sunny Sunday Morning

(c) Someone you admire

Improving your writing: verbs for effect

Skill definition: Selecting relevant and appropriate verbs to add to the atmosphere or meaning of your writing.

Choice of vocabulary is very important when writing, especially under timed conditions as you have a limited number of words to work with. Every word must count. Choosing verbs carefully is an effective way to add meaning to your work. You can do this by considering synonyms (words with the same or similar definitions) and picking the most appropriate one.

Look at the following list of words for 'walk':

| pace | amble | stroll | stride | march |

They each give a different image of how the person is moving.

- 'pace' suggests the walker has a purpose
- 'amble' suggests a slow speed and lack of direction
- 'stroll' suggests a walk for leisure or enjoyment
- 'stride' suggests long steps and confidence
- 'march' suggests speed, energy and perhaps a military setting

By understanding these shades of meaning, a single word can be used to give a considerable amount of information to the reader.

Train

1 Replace the underlined word in each of these sentences with a synonym.

   (a) She <u>took</u> the mysterious key in her hand.

   (b) She <u>went</u> to the shops quickly.

   (c) He <u>looked</u> at the birds with interest.

   (d) He <u>made</u> a beautiful model of a Viking ship.

   (e) We all <u>liked</u> the food in the restaurant.

2 Use a thesaurus to find a range of synonyms for the following verbs. Try to find at least ten each. List them in the order stated.

   (a) Run. List them in order of speed.

   (b) Say. List them in order of volume.

   (c) See. List them in order of how clearly they are seeing.

Test

Test time: 30:00

3 Write a short description of a race in which each participant is moving at a different speed. Use a range of verbs to convey this.

(25)

Improving your writing: choosing a point of view

Skill definition: Selecting an interesting and original point of view from which to write.

In many 11+ composition tasks, the question is quite open and allows you to make a range of choices about how you write. One way to make your writing stand out is to choose an unusual or different point of view to write from. In order to do this you need to consider the options you have for the given task. You will begin to think about this during the planning stages as you saw on pages 89–91.

Here are some ideas for different viewpoints:

- A narrator – this is a common choice for narrative writing.
- The main character – this means writing in the first person, for example, telling the story of *Peter Pan* from Peter's viewpoint.
- A minor character – this allows you to explore events from the point of view of someone else who is involved, for example, telling the story of *Peter Pan* from Wendy's point of view.
- A character who doesn't take part in the main story – this allows you to project what they might wonder or guess about what has happened, for example, telling the story of *Peter Pan* from his mother's point of view.
- An observer – this could be a human character or even an animal, for example, telling the story of *Peter Pan* from the crocodile's point of view.
- A character unrelated to the story, for example, a reporter writing for a newspaper about the events.

When writing from a different viewpoint you must think about:

- How does your storyteller feel about the events of the story?
- What is their opinion of what is happening?
- What knowledge do they have and what don't they know?
- What can their storytelling reveal about their own character?

Of course, the options you have depend on the task you are given and must still result in a satisfactory plot and a satisfactory ending. However, choosing a less obvious viewpoint can gain you more marks for content.

Train

1   From whose point of view could you re-tell these well-known stories?

   (a) 'Snow White and the Seven Dwarfs'   **(b)** *Harry Potter and the Chamber of Secrets*

   (c) 'The Three Little Pigs'   **(d)** 'Little Red Riding Hood'

   (e) *Charlie and the Chocolate Factory*   **(f)** 'The Hare and the Tortoise'

2   Think of a range of points of view for the following tasks:

   (a) The Escape   **(b)** Life Underground

   (c) A Day I'll Never Forget   **(d)** First came the crash, then came the silence …

Test

Test time: 30:00

3   Rewrite one of the well-known stories above from an alternative point of view.   (25)

Improving your writing: linking devices

Skill definition: Linking sentences and paragraphs together by using conjunctions.

Good planning should ensure that your writing is coherent and cohesive, that it makes sense and flows well. Another way to make certain that the various aspects of your writing link together is to use **conjunctions**. They ensure that your sentences follow on smoothly, one from the other, and that your paragraphs have some reference to each other. After all, you are writing one piece of work which should hold together for the reader. The ideas are divided into paragraphs but they should make sense as a whole.

Linking words and phrases

There are a range of words and phrases you can use to link ideas together. Below are some examples:

- Listing: firstly, secondly, thirdly, lastly
- Ordering: next, then, eventually, finally, in the end, to begin
- Emphasising: furthermore, moreover, also, above all, especially, in particular
- Showing similarity: similarly, likewise, equally, in the same way
- Showing difference: on the other hand, on the contrary, conversely, alternatively, instead
- Generalising: in general, largely, for the most part, usually, commonly
- Showing outcome: consequently, accordingly, therefore, thus
- Stating the obvious: obviously, of course, clearly, naturally
- Showing something unexpected: however, nonetheless, nevertheless, yet, still
- Summarising: in conclusion, in brief, overall

These devices can be used in both fiction and non-fiction writing. Some are quite formal and more suited to persuasive or discursive writing, others can be used in fiction writing but many can be used in both. Look in a book you are reading to see which you can find.

These words and phrases can be used within or between sentences to link ideas together. For example:

- Uniform should be compulsory, **however** occasional non-uniform days make for an interesting change.
- Omar climbed the stairs slowly **after** he had surveyed the hallway for anything unusual.
- He was immensely frightened and **moreover** he had good reason to be.
- Two thousand people signed the petition and it was sent to the local council. **Subsequently,** more recycling bins were placed in the town centre.

They can also be used to link paragraphs together. For example:

By and large, Kath was a well-behaved girl. She worked hard at school, she had many friends, she always helped out at home. Every morning she made her bed and every evening she did the washing up. Everybody thought she was an angel.

Nonetheless, Kath had a secret ... She was not the perfect child everybody assumed.

You should aim to use a range of these conjunctions throughout your writing.

Other ways to add cohesion

There are other ways to ensure cohesion in your writing without using linking words and phrases.

- Repetition – carefully repeating certain words to link different parts of the text together. Be careful not to overdo it. This is very common in speeches (see page 50).
- Mood – using description to keep the mood similar throughout the piece. Don't make sudden changes to a setting or a character.
- Full-circle planning – linking the end of your story back to the beginning to help it feel like one whole piece of writing.

Train ●

1   Imagine you are writing a letter to the Prime Minister asking him to ban cars in the centre of the town where you live. Write some sentences you might include in your letter using the following conjunctions:

- however
- nevertheless
- obviously
- eventually
- therefore

Test ● ● ● ● ● ● ● ● ● ● ● ● ● ● ● ● ● ●   Test time: 30:00

2   Write a letter to the Prime Minister, persuading him to ban cars from your town or city centre. Use conjunctions within your sentences and also between paragraphs to link your whole argument together.

(25)

Test 5: Composition

You have 30 minutes in which to choose, plan and write on ONE of the following. There are 25 marks are available.

1   Write a story using ONE of the following titles:
    - Guilty!
    - A Journey at Night
    - Opposite Sides

2   Write about a time when you felt that something was unfair.

3   Write a play script in which a child tries to persuade one of his or her parents to raise their pocket money.

4   'Children these days spend far too much time sitting in front of a computer screen.'

    Do you think that this is true?

    Give your opinions.

5   Write a letter to an inhabitant of another planet explaining what Christmas is.

6   Write about a book you have read which was set in a different time in history. Explain what it taught you about what life was like at that time.

7   'Look before you leap.' Use this as the starting point for a piece of writing.

8   Use this picture as a starting point for a piece of writing.

Record your score and time here and at the start of the book.

Score [ ] / 25   Time [ ] : [ ]

Test 6: Composition

You have 45 minutes in which to choose, plan and write on ONE of the following. There are 25 marks available.

1 Read the following paragraphs and then continue the story:

The Manor Museum of Natural History was very quiet that Saturday morning. The lady at the desk who sold the tickets looked bored and filed her nails. The guide whistled and looked for the umpteenth time at the notices on the wall. There had been no visitors yet.

But, in his lab at the back of the building, Professor Henry looked at his latest experiment and sighed.

2 Trouble at Sea

3 The Result

4 Practice Makes Perfect

5 Home Sweet Home

6 Magic

7 Look at this picture and create an imaginative composition based on it.

Record your score and time here and at the start of the book.

Score [ ] / 25 Time [ ] : [ ]

④ Useful information

Glossary of useful words and phrases

All of the following words and phrases are mentioned in this book. You should do your best to learn as many of the definitions as possible so that you are able to use the words with confidence and identify examples in exams.

Adjective – A word that describes a noun.
Adverb – A word that describes a verb. Adverbs often end in -ly.
Alliteration – A repeated letter or sound at the beginning of several words.
Antonym – A word that means the opposite.
Clause – A clause contains a subject and a verb. Clauses are the building blocks of sentences.
Complex sentence – A sentence that contains a main clause and a subordinate clause (see 'Subordinate clause' below).
Compound sentence – A sentence that is made up of two or more pieces of information joined by conjunctions.
Conjunction – A word that connects ideas within a sentence. Also known as a connective.
Contraction – A shortened word with the missing letters represented by an apostrophe.
Derivation – The source of a word, or where it comes from.
Dialogue – A conversation.
Direct speech – The exact words spoken by a character, written within "speech marks".
Embedded clause – A clause found in the middle of another clause, surrounded by commas.
Fiction – Writing that is made up/not true.
Figurative language – Language that is not literal and is used to achieve a particular effect.
Homonyms – Words that are spelled the same but have different meanings.
Homophones – Words that sound the same but are spelled differently.
Indirect speech – The general points of what someone has said but not the exact words spoken.
Main clause – A clause that makes sense on its own and can stand alone as a sentence.
Metaphor – A descriptive phrase that says something is something that it is not.
Non-fiction – A piece of writing that is factual.
Noun – A person, place or thing.
Onomatopoeia – The use of words that sound like the sound they are describing.
Paragraph – A section of writing/collection of sentences based on one subject.
Parts of speech – The group of words that a word belongs to according to its function, for example noun, adjective, adverb. Also known as word class.
Personification – Making something that is not a person sound like a person, for example, 'The trees whispered softly as Charlotte tiptoed through the glade.'
Persuasion – Making someone agree with you/share your views on a particular topic.
Phrase – A sequence of two or more words that does not contain a verb and its subject.
Prefix – A group of letters added to the beginning of a root word to change its meaning.
Preposition – A word that describes the location of something in relation to something else.
Pronoun – A word that can be used within a sentence to replace a noun.
Proper noun – The name of a specific person, place or thing, which needs a capital letter.
Root word – A basic word with no prefix or suffix added to it.
Simile – A phrase used to compare something to something else, using 'like' or 'as'.
Subject – The thing, person or idea that does or is something in a sentence.
Subordinate clause – A clause containing a subject and a verb, that does not make sense on its own, but adds information to a sentence.
Suffix – A group of letters added to the end of a word, changing or adding to its meaning. Suffixes can show which class a word belongs to.
Stanza – Another word for a verse.
Synonym – A word that has a similar meaning to another.
Tense – How to tell when an action took place.
Verb – An action or 'doing' word.

Advice for parents

The glossary list contains many terms with which your child should be familiar. To learn the list on their own would be very time-consuming and, for some children, a demoralising task. Learning the definitions by rote will not work for every child, but if they have worked through this book, they should have become familiar with the terms and what they mean.

In order to support your child, try to incorporate some of the terminology into your daily lives. If you see an example of a particular term or technique, make sure that you draw your child's attention to it. Looking out for examples in adverts and magazines and on cereal packets makes the ideas less abstract and more meaningful.

Never underestimate the importance of showing your child that what they learn at school has relevance outside the classroom in the real world. Similarly, asking your child to test you on the terms and giving wrong answers here and there so that they can correct you can be a huge morale boost for children who struggle to learn definitions.

Use these ideas to help your child learn the glossary words:

- Encourage your child to keep an English journal. Have a page for each major part of speech or piece of imagery (for example, verb, noun, simile, onomatopoeia) and collect examples from comprehension papers and books.
- When reading with your child, set challenges such as: find ten interesting verbs, guess how many pronouns are on this page (then count them), etc. Use these glossary words in context on a regular basis.
- Ask your child to write their own short grammar test for you using the relevant vocabulary. Get them to mark it and talk about the meanings of the words.
- Create pairs of cards with the glossary word on one card and an example on the other. Turn them all over and try to find pairs. Simply making the cards will help your child to learn the definitions.
- Come up with rhyming verses together to help your child remember difficult concepts, for example:

    The onomatopoeia train is coming down the track,
    With a dozen humming lamas and a score of grunting yaks...
    The buffet car is buzzing
    ...and the first class guests are 'zzing'
    As they run into the buffers with a very noisy THWACK!

Spelling list

All of the words on the list below are tricky for a particular reason. Some of them have silent letters, some have unstressed vowels, some have double letters and so on.

achieve	definite	irrelevant	quarter
acquire	describe	jealous	quiet
across	desperate	knowledge	receive
address	develop	length	recommend
advertise	difference	library	reference
advice	disappear	loneliness	rhythm
among	disappoint	losing	ridiculous
apparent	either	lying	safety
argument	embarrass	medicine	separate
awful	environment	minute	similar
balance	excellent	mysterious	sincerely
basically	except	necessary	soldier
becoming	exercise	neither	strength
beginning	explanation	occasion	succeed
believe	familiar	occurred	surely
benefit	fascinating	often	surprise
breathe	finally	original	temperature
brilliant	foreign	parallel	though
business	forty	particularly	through
careful	forward	peculiar	towards
certain	friend	perform	truly
chief	grammar	persuade	twelfth
coming	happiness	piece	until
competition	humorous	possess	usually
convenience	immediately	possible	weird
criticise	independent	probably	
decide	interesting	professional	

Advice for parents

There are many methods for learning spellings.

- The most commonly quoted is the **Look, Say, Cover, Write, Check, Look** method. This can be useful but it does not work for every child.

One thing you may find helpful is to identify what is tricky about the particular word and then devise your own way of remembering the correct spelling.

- **Mnemonics**: these are rhymes, phrases, diagrams or acronyms that can help your child to remember a spelling. Encourage your child to come up with a sentence or phrase where the initial letters of the words spell out the word they are finding hard to spell, for example, 'Big Elephants Can't Always Use Small Exits' for 'because'.
- **Phonetic pronunciation**: your child may find it easier to remember how to spell a word if they say it phonetically, for example, 'Wed-nes-day', 'me-rin-gue' or 'bis-cu-it'.
- **Words within words**: your child may find it easier to remember a word if they look for words they know inside words they don't know. They can think up a sentence that draws attention to it, for example, 'What a hat!' (for 'what'), or 'The e is at the end in friend' or 'There is a rat in "separate".'
- **Word families**: encourage your child to relate a new word to others with some common features, for example, familiar, family, famished.

Model writing samples

Here are some examples of writing by children in their first term of Year 6. They should give you an idea of what you should be aiming for. Some of the techniques used have been identified for you. All of these would gain extra marks in an exam.

Practice marking up your own writing in a similar way (on your own or with a parent), using different colours to identify key features that you are really proud of!

Extract 1

Here is an example of adventure narrative writing where the writer has tried to build tension in a variety of ways. Look at the annotations to see which techniques they have used.

use of senses   *short sentences help to create tension*   *sound*

The sea was encircling me. I was numb with fear. The shore was no more. The water crashed into the rocks, even though my only chance was to get to the rocks. I tried to gulp in air, but I ended up getting attacked by a salty wave. I tried to contain my fear, but waves of panic were drowning me. My throat was raw and dry, which seemed ironic, given my whereabouts.   *metaphor*

I thrashed about in the water, trying my level best to reach the rocks, but I couldn't. I felt as if a big sea-creature had sucked the life out of me. The light around me was dim. If I didn't reach the rocks soon, then hand in hand the darkness and the sea would swallow me up. My eyes stopped moving. My arms went rigid. My head lolled back.   *personification*

I took a few last wiggles of my fingers. The taste of blood trickled from my tongue. How had I got in to this mess? Was this what it was like to die?   *use of senses*

My head was thumping, my mind was racing. I could feel my heart beat at the edge of my chest. Every second I moved, every second I breathed, I was losing my will to live. The rocks kept looking further and further away.   *repetition for effect*

I coughed and spluttered. I sank below the surface. My determination had left me for good. My head felt empty and as the vast bubble of life left me, I wondered, would I live to see another day?

interesting verbs   *metaphor*

Daniel, Year 6

Extract 2

This example of writing is a short story based on a football match. Again the writer has built up tension in a variety of ways.

metaphor   *short sentences to help create tension*   *simile*   *metaphor*

I had been chosen. Me. For the penalty shot. Around me, the crowd was still as a wave of silence came over it. It was like a huge monster staring down at me with its thousands of pairs of eyes. I was an animal at the zoo, in the cage that held the last species left, fascinating everyone. The ball was on the spot and was luring me closer to it. As I looked up, the huge, fearsome goalie narrowed his eyes and gritted his teeth. At that moment, he was the person I felt the most hatred for in the world.   *interesting verbs*   *personification*   *interesting adjective*

I shuddered, wishing that one of my team-mates was in my place right now as I could not get the face of the goalie out of my mind. Grey clouds loomed over me, giving me a feeling of dread. 'I'm not going to do it, I'm not …'

Five seconds to go. The ref reached for his whistle.

Four – he grasped the cord.

Three – the metal dinked his chin. *interesting verb*

Two – he brought it towards his lips … *countdown creates tension*

One – he blew.

I pulled back my foot and felt the mud fly up. My foot paused as I noticed the little boy in the crowd fidgeting.

My foot hit the ball. *suspense – was it a goal?*

Megan, Year 6

Extract 3

This short narrative is in the mystery/horror genre. This is an obvious place to use tension in writing and it is done very effectively.

A rusty metal door opened with a high-pitched creak *sound*. A streak of light like a hand *simile* reached over to a small plump man. The floor was covered with old, empty bottles and hardened blood. The small, overweight man was slumped in a second-hand school chair. The man's head was pink and purple from all the alcohol he had consumed over the years. His grey suit was now as red as an African sunset *simile*. His thick moustache hung over his small upper lip.

"No," he whimpered, spit flying out of his dry mouth. "No, not you – anyone but you!" *interesting verbs*

"Be quiet," the shadow rasped. It had a thick Eastern European accent. Sweat was dripping down the chubby man's chalk-white forehead. His hands were now shaking uncontrollably, his bloodshot eyes darting from side to side.

The figure in the shadows flicked a switch. The chubby man winced. A lightbulb that hung from a tangled, flimsy wire turned on. The petrified man was stranded in the only light in the dim room.

The victim started to shake. He could hear knives being sharpened. He still had the image of the last time they did this to him.

He heard footsteps getting closer. His mind was racing, his heart pumping so fast it hurt. *interesting verb* The fat man tried to wriggle his over-size wrists out of the tight handcuffs. He saw the rusty door-knob twist. He winced. The door opened. Light flooded the room and a second figure loomed in the doorway with a knife in each fist. His huge feet sank in the ground as if he was walking through sinking sand *simile*. The obese man closed his eyes, his whole body shaking as though he were having a fit.

"Master," a low voice growled, and the knives changed hands and the dark shadow moved closer. The footsteps grew louder and louder. The clock in the corner clicked – the sound echoed round the room. The hands of the clock made the over-sized man think of two knives. *emphasises the spooky silence*

The shadow was getting closer. Inch by inch it came; it took its time because it knew its victim was defenceless.

Bottles were kicked out of the way. The fat man saw light glistening off the knives. The shadow was now a man with a harsh-looking face, two scars running down each cheek. *slowness add suspense* The obese man looked into the grey emotionless eyes of the man with the knives with little hope in his heart.

unpleasant detail *something nasty is about to happen!*

Oliver, Year 6

Extract 4

Here, the writer has described her neighbour; not only does she tell us facts about him, but she also comments on him. In this way, the writing does not turn into a list of facts about him, and is much more interesting.

Mr Brunger, our neighbour, thinks that it does not matter how old you are, you can always do as much as people much younger than you. He is 92. My mum was astonished *comment* when he told her he was going to America to give a talk on art. His lectures take him all over the world. He is a very interesting man, as you are about to find out. *comment* *comment*

He moved to London around 60 years ago with his wife Jean. He is a little eccentric; he cycles each day to the art gallery where he still works, his Sherlock Holmes cape flapping behind him. I would definitely call Mr Brunger a morning person. *comment* *comment*

You always know when he is going out because when he leads his bicycle out onto the road, the rusty brakes creak every time. Just before he gets on his battered bike he proudly puts on his deerstalker hat. He looks as though he is ready to venture into the jungle or go to war. I always wonder what he is thinking as he gazes into the distance before he sets off. *personification*

When I get home from school I see him at his desk reading a book on art or making notes for his next lecture. On the walls of his study, big portraits of his ancestors glare down at him.

His deafness makes him a little solitary; he tends to shout when he speaks to me.

Apart from his eccentricity he is one of the nicest neighbours anyone could have.

sound

comment

Macy, Year 6

Extract 5

In this example, a variety of persuasive techniques are used in a speech in favour of abolishing homework.

rhetorical questions

Do you enjoy homework? Do you want to get home from a long day and do yet more work? Students in the modern world are missing out on their childhood as they are overburdened with extra work in the evenings. *emotive language* *short sentences*

Everybody knows that your school days are the best days of your life. Memories. Friendships. New experiences. It would be a crime to sabotage those days with too much work, to steal away a young boy or girl's best years by forcing them to stay indoors doing sums or writing essays. Children should spend their afternoons playing, reading and relaxing. They need to spend quality time with their families and get plenty of sleep. Overloading them with homework prevents them from enjoying their time away from school. *persuasive language* *group of three*

Obviously education is paramount to every child but, on average, children spend eight hours a day at school. This is ample time to learn and practise the skills they require. Well-planned curriculums should allow students to complete all of the necessary work within the school day.

So teachers, hear our plea. Homework is outdated, outmoded and unnecessary. Unchain us from our desks, release us from our pen-and-paper shackles and allow us our freedom. *metaphors*

direct appeal to the reader

Ben, Year 6

Spelling, punctuation and grammar

You should aim to complete this test in 30 minutes.

There is a spelling mistake in each of these sentences. For each one, write down the letter that corresponds to the group of words containing the spelling mistake or, if there is no spelling mistake, write N for 'None'. There is 1 mark for each correct answer.

1   The man was very embarrased when his wig blew off in the wind.
    A   B   C   D   N

2   We are all going to the cinema exsept for your cousin.
    A   B   C   D   N

3   Our new teacher gave a very ntresting History lesson.
    A   B   C   D   N

4   I hit the ball too hard and it went straight threw the window.
    A   B   C   D   N

5   It is not usuall for you to be late to school.
    A   B   C   D   N

6   "This poem has a very distinct rythm," said the teacher to the class.
    A   B   C   D   N

7   The man apologised very sincerly for being late.
    A   B   C   D   N

8   He did not want to cause an arguement so quickly changed the subject.
    A   B   C   D   N

9   He swam fifty lenths of the pool in record time.
    A   B   C   D   N

10 "Is that really neccessary?" asked his mother tetchily.
    A   B   C   D   N

11 Mr Jones had built up a very successful busness selling shoes online.
    A   B   C   D   N

12 "I need you to be more definate about when you will be coming," she pleaded.
    A   B   C   D   N

13 "Can you reccommend a good book?" inquired Mary of the librarian.
    A   B   C   D   N

14 "Good grief, it's hot in here!" exclaimed John. "What on earth is the tempreture?"
    A   B   C   D   N

15 "My birthday is on the twelfth of May," said Jenny. "When's yours?"
    A   B   C   D   N   (15)

In this passage there are some mistakes in the use of capital letters and punctuation. On each numbered line there are two mistakes. Find the groups of words with the mistakes and write down their letters. (There are sometimes two mistakes within one letter, in which case you should write down the same letter twice.) Each correctly identified group is worth 2 marks.

16 "Excuse me," said katy to a passerby, "could you please direct me to the station"
      A   B   C   D

17 "of course," replied the kindly looking lady. "Its not far I promise you."
      A   B   C   D

18 Katy listened attentively. "Go to the end of this road and turn left said the lady.
       A   B   C   D

19 When you see a set of traffic lights, cross the road and keep walking in the same direction.
      A   B   C   D

20 katy smiled and nodded to show that she understood
    A   B   C   D

21 "Just as you go past the church it's a large church with a spire you will see an alleyway."
        A   B   C   D

22 alleyway, repeated Katy, to make sure she remembered.
    A   B   C   D

23 "Thats it. Just go up the alley and you will find the station.
    A   B   C   D

24 "Thank you very much, smiled Katy gratefully
    A   B   C   D

25 my pleasure," the lady replied amiably.
    A   B   C   D

(20)

Choose the best word (or pair of words) to complete this text so that it is written sensibly and in correct English. Circle the word, or group of words, that you have chosen. There is 1 mark for each correct answer.

26 Mrs Roberts looked round the classroom and sighed. **Because/Since/Although/Despite/ Whereas** she had been a teacher for over thirty years, this class was **different to/different from/unlike to/unlike from/disliked** any other she had ever **know/knew/knowed/was known/known**. They were the most messy, untidy group of children ever. They had gone out to the playground leaving the classroom looking **as like/like as/as though/as/though** a bomb had hit it.

Books **laid/laying/lying/lied/lay** on the floor, chairs were overturned, desks were covered with pieces of paper and a school scarf was **hung/hanging from/hung to/hanging about/ hanging to** one of the lights. 'Right,' she said to herself, 'I've **have/will have/haven't/won't/ had** enough of this. As soon as they come back I will make them clear **out/up/down/over/ off** this mess. And to stop them doing it again, they can jolly well **remainder/reminder/ remind/remained/remain** in the classroom for the whole of the lunch break and **written/ wrote/writing/will write/write** me a letter of apology.'

(10)

27 Rewrite this passage, correcting the errors of spelling, punctuation and grammar.

when you go to the theater today you expect a roof over your head warmth comftable seats and peace and quite in shakespeares day it was not like this at all. If you were not well off you got wet on a rainy day you would be standing and get jostled by apple-sellers you would chat to your neighbours and hiss or cheer the actors you could look up at those richer than you who sat with a small roof over their heads on dry seats they in turn looked enviosly at the noblemen and women who sat above the stage in the best seats of all on stage, boy actors took the parts of young girls and older men played the wommen for not until long after shakespeare died was it thought proper for femails to appear on stage.   (15)

Record your score and time here and at the start of the book.

Score ⬜ / 60   Time ⬜ : ⬜

Comprehension 1

In this multiple-choice test, answer each question by writing down the letter that is next to the correct answer. Give only one answer for each question. If you make a mistake, rub it out first and then write down your new answer.

You should aim to finish all the questions, but if you are finding a question difficult, do not waste time, just move on to the next question. If you are unsure of an answer, it is better to mark one than none at all.

Read the passage carefully and work as quickly as you can. You should aim to complete the test in 23 minutes. This includes five minutes' reading time.

This passage comes from Nigel Slater's autobiography *Toast – The story of a boy's hunger*. In the book, Slater, who is now a famous chef, tells the story of his childhood, through food. Each section of the book has a type of food as its title.

Peach flan

Mrs Muggeridge was a short, solid, black woman. It wasn't her skin that was black, it was her soul. In the six weeks she spent as our cleaner she never smiled once. She would shoo me away like a pesky fly. A woman steeped in vinegar. A hairy mole on her chin did her no favours.

5   Mrs Muggeridge was more than a cleaner. When my mother was in bed, too weak to cook, she would make lunch for me. If ever there was a meal seasoned with hatred this was it. Hatred for a life that saw her scrubbing people's lavatories for a living; hatred for having to feed a fussy little boy when she could have none of her own; hatred for the sirloin steak she grilled for my Monday lunches while she would go home to boiled neck of fatty lamb
10 and carrots.

    We never found out her Christian name. I'm not sure she even had one. It wouldn't surprise me if she had been christened Mrs Muggeridge. For all this, her cooking had a spring in its step. Her peas were green not grey, her pork chops were not brown and dry like Mother's but salty outside and juicy within. Her flapjacks were soft and crumbly not
15 brittle. On Fridays she would make a fruit flan – tinned peaches and a cocktail cherry on a yellow sponge base.

    One morning when I was off school with one of the bilious attacks that came so conveniently before maths tests, she showed me how to make the peach flan. The sponge base came from a packet, the peaches from a tin. But she let me arrange the slices in the
20 sponge case, neatly overlapping one on another. She produced the cherry from the tissue in her apron pocket. I put it exactly in the centre. We opened a sachet of Quick-Gel and mixed it with hot water. As soon as the red gunge started to cool I spooned it over the fruit. It set in seconds. There it was, a great orange and red wheel. I wanted to take it upstairs to show my mother but Mrs Muggeridge wouldn't let me. The wait for my father to come
25 home for lunch was interminable. I wanted to see his face when he saw what I'd made.

    "Don't be nosy," she snapped when I asked her what her husband did, trying to fill a silence. "He isn't around any more. I've had to do without him for a year now. Just like you are going to have to do without your mother."

    That night, as he was tucking me into bed, I asked my father what she meant by "just like
30 you are going to have to."

    I never saw Mrs Muggeridge or her peach flan again.

1 What does the author describe as black in the opening paragraph? (1)

A Mrs Muggeridge's skin

B Mrs Muggeridge's hair

C Mrs Muggeridge's house

D Mrs Muggeridge's soul

E Mrs Muggeridge's clothes

2 Which phrase from the opening paragraph tells us that Mrs Muggeridge did not enjoy the author's company? (1)

A 'she never smiled once'

B 'A woman steeped in vinegar'

C 'a hairy mole on her chin did her no favours'

D 'She would shoo me away like a pesky fly'

E None of these

3 What does the phrase 'a woman steeped in vinegar' tell us about Mrs Muggeridge? (1)

A she smells of vinegar

B she uses vinegar in her cooking

C she works in a fish and chip shop

D she is a sour, unpleasant woman

E she is tall

4 What does the sentence 'A hairy mole on her chin did her no favours' mean? (1)

A the mole was not helpful to her cleaning work

B the mole was unpleasant

C the mole was her pet

D the mole needed to be removed

E the mole didn't help her to seem like a nice person

5 What else did Mrs Muggeridge do in addition to cleaning? (1)

A cooking

B ironing

C washing

D nursing

E teaching

6 Of which literary technique is 'a meal seasoned with hatred' an example? (1)

A simile

B metaphor

C alliteration

D onomatopoeia

E repetition

7 According to the passage, which two things does Mrs Muggeridge hate? (1)

A a and e   a fussy children

B a and c   b cooking

C b and d   c her life

D d and e   d lamb

E b and e   e seasoning food

8 Which piece of evidence shows that the author's family have more money than Mrs Muggeridge? (1)

A they eat tinned peaches

B the author has days off school

C Mrs Muggeridge's peas were green

D the author has sirloin steak for lunch

E Mrs Muggeridge makes peach flan

9 Which piece of evidence suggests that Mrs Muggeridge is a better cook than the author's mother? (1)

A her peas were green, not grey

B her pork chops were juicy within

C her flapjacks were soft and crumbly

D none of these

E answers a, b and c

10 Based on your reading of the text, which of the following sentences are definitely true? (1)

A Mrs Muggeridge did not have a Christian name

B She had a mole on her cheek

C She is a bad cook

D Her husband is no longer around

E She likes fussy children

11 Which of these best explains the meaning of 'her cooking had a spring in its step'. (1)

A Mrs Muggeridge used spring vegetables in her cooking

B She liked to cook unusual things

C Her cooking was interesting and tasty

D She only cooked greens

E Her cooking leapt across the room

12 Which of the following best describes how Mrs Muggeridge planned the meals? (1)

A there was something new every day

B she served the same foods on certain days

C she liked to experiment with ingredients

D she asked the author what he wanted to eat

E she cooked the same as she had at home

13 According to the author, what was the reason that he stayed at home on the day that he made peach flan? (1)

   A a bilious attack

   B his mother was unwell

   C he didn't like school

   D his father wouldn't let him go to school

   E Mrs Muggeridge told him off

14 Which word tells us that the author was *not* genuinely unwell when he had the day off school? (1)

   A bilious

   B brittle

   C conveniently

   D overlapping

   E attacks

15 What substance holds the peaches inside the flan? (1)

   A custard

   B hot water

   C flapjack

   D cocktail cherries

   E jelly

16 What shape is the flan? (1)

   A triangular

   B round

   C square

   D there is no evidence about its shape

   E oval

17 What is the most likely reason for Mrs Muggeridge preventing the author from showing his mother the flan? (1)

   A she does not like his mother

   B she wants to keep the flan for herself

   C his mother is allergic to peaches

   D she does not want him to disturb his mother

   E she is embarrassed by the flan

18 What is the meaning of the word 'interminable'? (1)

   A boring

   B unending

   C interesting

   D frequent

   E impatient

19 Why does the author want to see his father's face when he shows him the flan? (1)

    A   the author is proud of what he has made

    B   his father is very fond of flan

    C   he has not seen his father for a long time

    D   his father has a nice face

    E   the author is taller than his father

20 Based on what you have read, what do you think is the most likely reason that the author never saw Mrs Muggeridge or her peach flan again? (1)

    A   Mrs Muggeridge died

    B   the author's father did not like the flan

    C   Mrs Muggeridge found another job

    D   the author's father fired her for suggesting that the author's mother was going to die

    E   the author choked on the flan

Comprehension 2

Read the passage and answer as many of the questions as you can. If you find a question too difficult, go on to the next one and come back to the difficult question at the end. You may make notes around the passage if you wish. You should aim to complete the test in 45 minutes.

This extract is from *A Flight of Swans* by Barbara Willard. Humphrey Jolland is fifteen years old and is travelling to his relations. He is in the care of Robin Medley. The story is set in the sixteenth century just as the Spanish fleet has come to attack the English in the Channel.

There was a sound below. Someone was crossing the yard towards the stable. Humphrey sat up in the straw, troubled lest the rustling should wake Robin. He must have slept himself more than he supposed, for the faint light of very early morning showed him an outline or two. As he sat there, summoning his courage for the next move, his heart
5 unpleasantly thumping, a cock crew far away and the first blackbird sounded sleepily among the laden trees in the orchard behind the inn.

The horses stamped and stirred below, blowing softly – and then almost immediately one of them gave a faint whinny. A man – no, two men, talking softly – came into the stable. A light showed Humphrey the square of the open trap, swinging, then steadying as the
10 lantern was hung. The pair who had entered spoke in quiet voices that befitted the hour, yet somehow gave an impression of secrecy, of urgency. Straw rustled underfoot as they moved to their horses; leather creaked; metal jingled. They were preparing to saddle up.

Humphrey wormed his way cautiously across the floor and lay peering down through the trap, straining to hear what was being said. The coast … quite certainly something
15 about the coast … Humphrey almost fell down the ladder in his eagerness.

"The ostler says we'd have done better to ride by Horsham," one man said.

"They were all drunk. What good's a sot's advice?"

"Well, we're halfway to the coast by now, whichever the road." His horse stamped, and tossed against the bit. "Easy now. Be still, you damned brute," he said, but softly and
20 lovingly.

"Only let 'em dally till we come!" cried the second man, laughing. "That's all I pray for."

"Amen to that – for as I see it, once they're into the Straits there's little hope of a good showing. They might battle all day and we'd do no better than hear their guns!"

Humphrey was shaking with excitement. This was such good fortune he could hardly
25 contain himself in silence. Here were two of those gentry he and Robin had seen riding out of London in their tens and scores, intent only on getting to the coast and from some imagined point watching the great men-of-war beating up the channel, with Howard and Drake and Hawkins pressing on their heels. Few of them had any great notion of the width of the waters, and some of them innocently supposed they might take a pot at the enemy
30 on their own account ... From the first sight of them, Humphrey had only one thing in mind – to give Robin the slip and join these hopeful travellers.

Now here was opportunity actually within sight.

The two in the stable below were young and well-dressed – acceptable gallants not sly adventurers. Humphrey let himself down a few rungs of the ladder. Immediately, the taller
35 of the two looked up and called out.

"So there's a lad or two still living in this forsaken hovel! Give a hand here, boy – the landlord's as drunk as all the rest or we'd have had him out of his bed."

Humphrey replied coldly, "I am a traveller, sir, as you are." He let himself down the remaining rungs and stood as haughtily as he knew how – and he was, as his cousin Ursula
40 Medley, Robin's wife, had said, "a stomachy lad."

The young man grimaced and then laughed. "I do beg your pardon, my dear good young gentleman. For all that – pray pocket your dignity and give a hand."

Humphrey held the horse's head, while its master saw to the girths.

"Do you ride to the coast, sirs? Do you ride to see the Spanish ships?"

1 Explain the effect of the following words or phrases used by the author:

   (a) 'his heart unpleasantly thumping' (1)

   (b) 'Humphrey wormed his way cautiously across the floor' (1)

2 How are the men feeling about the fight with the Spanish? Use evidence from the text to support your answer. (2)

3 In this passage, Humphrey is very eager to join the men in their fight against the Spanish. Find an example that shows this and explain your views on his eagerness. (3)

4 Explain, in your own words, the meaning of the following phrase: 'pray pocket your dignity.' (1)

5 What sort of person did the two men think Humphrey was? How do you know? (2)

6 Explain, fully and in your own words, why the young man laughed in the penultimate paragraph. (3)

7 Give three examples to show that this story is set a long time ago. (3)

8 Why do you think Humphrey wanted to get away from Robin? (3)

9 Write the next paragraph of the story, continuing the conversation that Humphrey has with the men. Remember to include direct speech and to use a style as similar to the original as you can. (6)

Record your score and time here and at the start of the book.

Score ☐ / 25   Time ☐ ☐ : ☐

Composition 1

You should spend 30 minutes on this test, including planning time.

Write on any ONE of the following topics. Each one is worth 25 marks. You should think of your own title for questions 1, 4, 6 and 7. Question 2 does not need a title.

1   Write a story that begins with the following:

    Clink! I landed in the bottom of an old hat and nestled in the damp, brown folds, along with some other coins. There were quite a few like me …

2   Write a story that includes an argument between two people.

3   Pre-Match Nerves

    Interpret this title in an imaginative way.

4   Write a description of ONE of the following:

    • a crowded beach

    • a dentist's waiting room

    • a secluded lake

5   My Moment of Glory

    Create a composition with this theme.

6   Write about a character in a book who has inspired you in some way. Explain what he/she does in the book that inspires you.

7   Write in any way you like about this picture.

Composition 2

You should spend 30 minutes on this test, including planning time.

Write on any ONE of the following topics. Each one is worth 25 marks. You should think of your own title for questions 3, 6 and 7. Questions 1 and 5 do not need a title.

1 Write a speech in which you try to persuade members of your class to support a particular charity. Be sure to say something about what the charity does.

2 Being Different

3 Write a description of ONE of the following:
   - an exotic marketplace
   - a stormy sea
   - a garden at night

4 My Most Valued Possession

5 Write about a character in a book whom you really disliked. Be sure to say why you found this person so horrible.

6 Write a story that contains the sentence: 'The sorcerer sighed.'

7 Write in any way you like about this picture.

Success grids

For narrative writing, personal response, letters, responding to pictures and textual prompts

What the examiners will be looking for, in order of importance:	Marks available: 25
Content, purpose and organisation: Is your composition engaging and interesting for the reader? Does it hold their attention? Have you used a balance of narration, description, dialogue and action when writing a story? Have you done as the title instructed? Have you spent most of your time on the main point behind the title? If you are responding to a picture or text prompt, have you interpreted the stimulus imaginatively? Is your idea original? Have you used paragraphs to separate the beginning, middle and end? Have you used verb tenses correctly? (For example, if you have started writing in the past tense, you should make sure that you have not drifted into using the present tense by mistake.) Does your opening sentence get the reader interested? Is your last sentence a clear ending? If you have written a letter, have you set it out correctly?	10
Language: Does your language match that of the kind of person who is speaking – or being spoken to? (For example, if you are pretending to be an important adult, you need to sound like one; if you are writing a letter to an important adult, you need to use more formal language than you would normally use.) Have you used interesting and adventurous vocabulary? Check your choice of verbs ('ambled' tells us more than 'went'), adjectives and adverbs. Have you used 'writers' tricks' such as metaphors and similes to make your writing more interesting and put a clear picture into the head of the reader?	5
Style: Have you used a good mixture of simple, compound and complex sentences? Have you started your sentences in a range of ways, using adverbs, conjunctions, -ing or -ed words to avoid repetition? Have you remembered to include the thoughts and feelings of characters (instead of just saying what they did and what happened to them)? Have you varied the pace of your writing by using different lengths of sentences?	5
Spelling, punctuation and grammar: Have you used a range of punctuation including commas, exclamation marks, ellipses and speech marks (where appropriate)? Is your spelling of common words accurate? Is your spelling of complex words logical and reasonable? Do your sentences make sense when you read them back? Are your verb tenses correct? Have you missed out any words? Have you written in proper sentences?	5

For continuing a story

What the examiners will be looking for, in order of importance:	Marks available: 25
Content, purpose and organisation: Have you written a logical and appropriate continuation? Have you picked up on any clues in the original text which suggest what might happen next? Have you kept the same characters and do they speak and act in the same way as in the original? Have you kept the same pace as in the original? Your continuation should last as long in time as the original. For example, if the passage you read lasted around one hour of the characters' lives, you should write about the next hour. Have you started directly after the original text finished? Have you used paragraphs to separate the beginning, middle and end? Have you written in the same tense and person as the original text? Does your opening sentence get the reader interested? Is your last sentence a clear ending?	10
Language: Have you used similar language to the original text? Have you used interesting and adventurous vocabulary? Check your choice of verbs ('ambled' tells us more than 'went'), adjectives and adverbs. Have you used 'writers' tricks' such as metaphors and similes to make your writing more interesting and put a clear picture into the head of the reader?	5
Style: Have you used a good mixture of simple, compound and complex sentences? Have you started your sentences in a range of ways, using adverbs, conjunctions, -ing or -ed words to avoid repetition? Have you varied the pace of your writing by using different lengths of sentences? If the original author used dialogue, have you used dialogue? If the original author used plenty of description, have you used plenty of description?	5
Spelling, punctuation and grammar: Have you used a range of punctuation including commas, exclamation marks, ellipses and speech marks (where appropriate)? Is your spelling of common words accurate? Is your spelling of complex words logical and reasonable? Do your sentences make sense when you read them back? Are your verb tenses correct? Have you missed out any words? Have you written in proper sentences?	5

For writing about a book you have read

What the examiners will be looking for, in order of importance:	Marks available: 25
Purpose and organisation: Have you done as the title instructed? Have you spent most of your time on the main point behind the title? Have you included details of *your response* to the book? Have you used paragraphs to separate each idea? Have you used verb tenses correctly? (If you have started writing in the past tense, you should make sure that you have not drifted into using the present tense by mistake.) Have you re-told the story? Remember, you should *not* have done so! Unless the title tells you to focus on only one of the following, have you remembered to mention characters, plot, setting and structure?	10
Language: Have you used clear, simple language to get across the points you want to make? Have you used 'book' language such as author, chapter, plot, etc.? Have you described your response or opinion using book-related vocabulary, such as unputdownable, gripping, slow-paced, lacking in depth, etc., rather than general comments?	5
Style: Have you used a good mixture of simple, compound and complex sentences? Have you started your sentences in a range of ways, using adverbs, conjunctions, -ing or -ed words to avoid repetition? Have you used similes or metaphors to describe the book or your reaction to it?	5
Spelling, punctuation and grammar: Have you used a range of punctuation including commas, exclamation marks, semicolons, etc.? Is your spelling of common words accurate? Is your spelling of complex words logical and reasonable? Do your sentences make sense when you read them back? Are your verb tenses correct? Have you missed out any words? Have you written in proper sentences?	5

For discursive and persuasive writing

What the examiners will be looking for, in order of importance:	Marks available: 25
Purpose and organisation: Have you done as the title instructed and kept to the point? Have you made an equal number of points for and against in a discursive piece? Is your message consistent in a persuasive piece? Have you used paragraphs to separate each point? Have you given an example to illustrate each point? Does your opening sentence get the reader (or listener) interested? Is your last sentence a clear ending? If it is a speech, have you summed up what you have said at the end?	10
Language: Is your language clear and to the point? Remember that the opening sentence of each paragraph should clearly state the point you are making. Have you used 'writers' tricks' such as metaphors and similes to make your writing more interesting and put a clear picture into the head of the reader? Have you used a range of persuasive phrases if appropriate? Have you used conjunctions to link your ideas together?	5
Style: Have you used a good mixture of simple, compound and complex sentences? Have you started your sentences in a range of ways, using adverbs, conjunctions, -ing or -ed words to avoid repetition? Have you used formal language?	5
Spelling, punctuation and grammar: Have you used a range of punctuation including commas, semicolons, colons and brackets? Is your spelling of common words accurate? Is your spelling of complex words logical and reasonable? Do your sentences make sense when you read them back? Are your verb tenses correct? Have you missed out any words? Have you written in proper sentences?	5

Answers

1 Spelling, punctuation and grammar

Prefixes (page 14)

<u>Train</u>

1 Answers will vary. For example:
   - (a) submarine
   - (b) prepare
   - (c) revisit
   - (d) antiviral
   - (e) impossible

2 (a) ad – to/towards. For example, advance
   (b) extra – beyond/outside. For example, extraordinary
   (c) over – excessive/above. For example, override
   (d) semi – half/partial. For example, semicircle
   (e) under – below/beneath. For example, undergrowth

3 (a) **out**ran
   (b) un**acceptable**
   (c) mis**understood**
   (d) extra**ordinary**
   (e) im**possible**
   (f) ir**regular**

<u>Test</u>

4 I tried to open the door but it was **im**possible. The handle was broken and **im**mobile. I wanted to try and break it down but that would be **il**legal. What could I do to **pro**gress on my journey? I was feeling **im**patient so I picked up a brick to smash the window but something made me **re**think it. I was **un**prepared for this problem. I **re**traced my steps to the front of the house and noticed something **extra**ordinary. An open window. I had finally **dis**covered/**un**covered a way in. (1 mark each)

Suffixes (page 16)

<u>Train</u>

1 (a) slipped/slipping
   (b) tripped/tripping
   (c) tapped/tapping
   (d) pardoned/pardoning
   (e) clipped/clipping

2 betrayed, smelliest, curliest, muddiest, replying, juiciness

3 (a) accelerating, accelerated
   (b) assuming, assumed
   (c) excluding, excluded
   (d) finer, finest
   (e) stranger, strangest
   (f) gentler, gentlest
   (g) simpler, simplest

4 It was the **hottest** day on record and Jane had **stopped skipping** in the park because she was **sweaty** and thirsty. She **flopped** onto the grass and **sipped** on her water. She felt **sleepy** so closed her droopy eyelids and **dozed** off. When she awoke, her eyes gradually **fixed** on the figure standing before her.

5 (a) happiness
   (b) government
   (c) illness
   (d) amusement
   (e) improvement
   (f) fitness
   (g) foolishness
   (h) heaviness
   (i) sadness
   (j) loneliness

6 (a) **Various** people have climbed the **mountainous** regions of Nepal.
   (b) The comedian was very **humorous**.
   (c) The cost of the holiday was **outrageous**.

7 Answers will vary. For example:
   (a) The pianist played **brilliantly**.
   (b) Every evening I **carefully** complete my homework.
   (c) This year my exam results were **considerably** better than last year.
   (d) **Sadly** it is nearly time to go to school.

<u>Test</u>

8 Suddenly, the ship **swayed** from side to side, **battling** the enormous waves. The **courageous** captain **controlled** the sails and the crew **rallied** together to bail out the water. The **choppiness** of the water worsened and the boat **tipped** over **dangerously**. There was no **merriment** aboard that day. Everyone **frantically** worked to survive. (1 mark each)

Plurals and silent letters (page 20)

1 (a) Answers will vary.
   (b) Answers will vary. For example, scissors, trousers

2 (a) desperate
   (b) generous
   (c) interesting
   (d) jewellery
   (e) subtle
   (f) knowledgeable
   (g) soften
   (h) answer
   (i) wrangle
   (j) knead
   (k) mortgage

3 Arthur was out **jogging** one morning. As he ran he took in the **scenery** and found himself growing **envious** of the beautiful houses and gardens he passed along his route. He looked at his watch. His face was **solemn** when he realised that his time was slower than the day before. **Disappointed**, he **hastened** to make up the lost time by sprinting for the next five hundred metres but he suddenly felt an agonising pain in his left **knee**. As he hobbled towards the park he saw a small dog **exploring** the undergrowth. It seemed **unnatural** for a dog to be in the park without an owner in sight at this **hour** of the day.   (1 mark each)

Homophones, homonyms and other commonly confused words (page 22)

Train

1 (a) morning – before lunch; mourning – sadness at grief
  (b) principal – leader of an organisation; principle – a fundamental truth
  (c) passed – past tense of pass; past – before now
  (d) allowed – permitted; aloud – able to be heard
  (e) alter – to change; altar – a table used for religious offerings
  (f) compliment – a nice comment; complement –something that matches or fits in
  (g) hole – a void; whole – entire
2 (a) long – not short/to yearn
  (b) back – spine/behind
  (c) match – a firelighter/a contest in sport/to fit in or be the same as
  (d) left – remaining/direction opposite of right
  (e) right – correct/direction opposite of left/something you are entitled to
  (f) leaves – plural of leaf/goes away
  (g) rose – a flower/moved upwards
  The sentences written using these words will vary.
3 (a) dairy – where milk is produced / diary – a written record of somebody's life
  (b) stationery – pens, pencils, etc. / stationary – not moving
  (c) precede – to come before / proceed – to go forwards
  (d) licence – a document giving permission to do something / license – to give a licence
  The sentences written using these words will vary.

Test

4 Once **there** was a **bear** who lived in the woods. He was a very grumpy bear because he had tripped over a **loose** rock and **now** he had a **sore** toe. The plaster he had used had stuck **to** his **fur**. To make himself feel better he **made** a sandwich but his foot was still hurting so he decided to phone the doctor. The receptionist told him he **would** have to **wait** a **week for** an appointment when the doctor would be able to **advise** him on what to do. When he **heard** this the bear could not **accept** that he would have to **be** patient. He didn't **know whether** to scream **aloud** or **groan** quietly. "**Great**," he growled as he slammed down the phone. The only thing he could think to do now was eat **some dessert** to cheer himself up before it was **past** his bedtime.   (1 mark for each)

Basic punctuation (page 24)

Train

1 Punctuation is very important to writers. It helps them to divide their writing into sentences and to ensure that what they want to say is clear and can be understood. The writing of authors such as Charles Dickens and William Shakespeare would be impossible to understand without punctuation. Their stories have been translated into many languages, including French and Russian, and these languages also use punctuation. Without it we would be very confused.
2 (a) Who is responsible for protecting our environment?
  (b) Hurry up!
  (c) What a fantastic result!
  (d) Are you sure you want to go to James' house?
  (e) I wondered if I should stay at home or go to the party.

Test

3 Kaya could see exotic fruits and vegetables on every market stall. The smells were enticing and her stomach began to rumble. What an amazing sight! She could not quite believe that planet Earth could produce so much incredible produce. What should she try first? She was so excited to be in Brazil and could not wait to experience all it had to offer. Where to begin?   (1 mark for each correction)

Commas and apostrophes (page 26)

Train

1 Answers will vary but should use commas correctly. For example: When I am older I would like to be a police officer, a doctor, a lawyer, a vet or a teacher.
2 Answers will vary but should use commas correctly. For example: Every Sunday afternoon, Amar went to the cinema.
3 Answers will vary but should use commas correctly. For example: Alfie, who practised every day, passed his violin exam.
4 I won't be able to go Sam's party. He'll be twelve years old on Thursday. I'll be sad to miss it because his mum's cooking is always delicious. The cake's icing is soft and the pizza's crust is crispy. The drinks are always fizzy and his brother James plays good music. James' speakers are really loud!

Test

5 It contains a list. (1 mark)
6 The commas separate the clause. (1 mark)
7 Chris, who was revising for his exams, made a timetable for his bedroom wall. It showed which subjects he had to revise, when he had time to revise and which books he would need to use. He was organised, efficient, enthusiastic and his dad was proud of all the hard work he was putting in. (5 marks)
8 Possession – it shows that the boys own the coats. (1 mark)
9 The first is a contraction (it is) and the second is possession (the party belongs to Sarah). (1 mark for each)
10 Carolyn's favourite place to visit is the zoo. She loves to see the monkeys jumping around their trees and the elephants' huge trunks spraying water. She always visits when the penguins are being fed so that she can see the other people's reactions. She's also a fan of the aquarium and its multicoloured fish but she doesn't like the reptile house. The snakes' beady eyes are a bit frightening. (6 marks)

Parentheses (page 29)

Train

1 Answers will vary. For example: Helen, who was tall and skinny like a lamppost, squeezed through the gap in the fence.

Test

2 Cats, which are one of the most popular pets in this country, are friendly and lovable companions. Most people (over 75 per cent according to a study) would like to have a pet. Different breeds offer different benefits. Some stay indoors – such as Persians – and others – such as Ragdolls – like to adventure outdoors. Everyone in the family, both young and old, will enjoy having a feline companion. (10 marks)

Punctuating speech (page 30)

Train

1 It was the night before my sister's birthday and Mum and I were in the kitchen, frantically baking a cake.
"Get me the butter from the fridge!" screamed Mum in a panic.
"I can't find it," I replied. "Which shelf is it on?"
"I don't know. Use your eyes," she retorted. Finally I found it and gave it to Mum. Just as I did she knocked the flour off the counter and all over the floor.
"Look what you've done now!" she yelled. She was covered in flour from head to toe. There was silence for a minute then we both burst out laughing.
"Would it be better to buy a cake at the supermarket?" asked Mum.

Test

2 A (1 mark)
3 C (1 mark)
4 E (1 mark)
5 N (1 mark)
6 D (1 mark)

Colons, semicolons and ellipses (page 32)

Train

1 (a) He wrote a short list for Santa: a red bike, a new pencil case and a book about dinosaurs.
(b) He couldn't answer the teacher: he had completely forgotten the question.
(c) For the exam you will need the following items: a black pen, a 30cm ruler, a sharp pencil and an eraser.
(d) His hard work paid off: the concert was a success.
(e) The head teacher made an announcement: the netball match was cancelled.

2 Answers will vary. For example:
   (a) Exercising is important; it keeps your heart healthy.
   (b) It is not easy to learn to drive; there are lots of skills to apply at once.
   (c) Books make wonderful presents; everybody likes a good story.
3 Answers will vary, but ellipses should be used correctly.

Test

4 Sam was happy: he had finally finished his homework. He had piles of it this weekend: French, Science, Maths,
   Geography and History. It seemed unfair. His brother didn't have any homework; he was playing on his laptop. His
   sister didn't have any homework; she was playing outside on the swings. Being the oldest was tough but he hoped all
   the hard work would pay off. Eventually ...   (1 mark for each correction)

Types of sentences and clauses (page 34)

Train

1 Answers will vary.
2 (a) Lucinda, **who was an excellent gymnast**, won three medals in yesterday's competition.
   (b) **As it was raining**, I took my umbrella.
   (c) The schoolchildren ran across the playground, **as they laughed their heads off**.
3 Answers will vary.
4 Answers will vary.

Test

5 Answers will vary. For example: My sister, Maisie, is four years old. She likes dancing and swimming but sometimes
   she annoys me by taking my toys without asking. Her best friend, who is called Freya, lives next door. They like to
   play on the trampoline in our garden; it's huge. Maisie and Freya make lots of noise and they love playing together.
   I wish I had a brother – we could play with dinosaurs. Maisie does not like dinosaurs because she says they are silly.
   I don't think they are silly: I like them. (1 mark for each sentence that has been changed to a maximum of 10 marks)

Parts of speech (page 36)

Train

1 Answers will vary. For example:
   (a) The brown dog ran quickly across the public park and started to dig furiously under the tallest tree.
   (b) The elegant ship glided peacefully over the still water with the wind in its white sails.
   (c) The shiny car drove speedily through the deserted town and parked badly outside the grand house.
2 Answers will vary. For example:
   (a) Dad went **to** the supermarket **because** we had run out of milk.
   (b) I found my slippers **under** the sofa **but** it was the last place I looked.
   (c) I heard the car coming **behind** me **so** I waited before I crossed the road.
3 (a) Lisa took **her** dog for a walk in the park because **he** had been indoors all day.
   (b) Mark walked into the classroom, **he** found an empty seat and sat down.
   (c) Sian's mother told **her** to go to the shops to buy milk because **she** had run out.
4 (a) I **set (verb)** the table with our new **set (noun)** of cutlery.
   (b) Can somebody sitting **close (adjective)** to the door please **close (verb)** it?
   (c) It would only be **fair (adjective)** if everybody rode the merry-go-round at the **fair (noun)**.
   (d) My good mood will **last (verb)** until the end of the day as long as I don't come **last (adjective)** in the race.

Test

5 Three from: was, skipped, thought, saw, chatting, laughing, had, been, get, seeing, spotted, sprinting, jumped,
   clipped, tumbled, exclaimed, erupted, started, giggle, known, are, looked, spent, hadn't, seen, said, helped(1 mark each)
6 Three from: merrily, loudly, helplessly, forever   (1 mark each)
7 Pronoun   (1 mark)
8 Pronoun   (1 mark)
9 Proper noun   (1 mark)
10 Three from: along, through, into, towards, over, onto, from, at, in   (1 mark each)

Test 1: Spelling, punctuation and grammar (page 38)

Answers are worth 1 mark unless otherwise indicated.

1 As Simon **grabbed** his bag and ran out of the **building** he could still hear his teacher's words **echoing** in his head. He
   could not **describe** how **embarrassed** he was at being told off in front of all of his **friends**. He shook his head in **disbelief**.
   He hadn't even done anything *that* **unpleasant** this time! It had just **occurred** to him, halfway through the morning, that
   this **particular** science lesson was a bit boring. It needed someone to make it a bit more **exciting**. Mr Jones was being
   extremely unreasonable about it all. It was just a few chemicals. He hadn't intended to blow a hole in the wall so that

everyone could see **straight** through it into the **library**. He had put on his most **solemn** face and **apologised** but Mr Jones had **immediately** taken the **necessary** precautions, removed him from the classroom and sent him **directly** to the Headmaster's office. Mr Watkins had decided to **ensure** that this type of unruly **behaviour** never happened again. He had marched Simon back into the classroom and told him off for a full five **minutes** in front of the whole class. He had then excluded him from school for a week. Simon felt the **familiar** feeling of dread as he trudged home **slowly**. (25 marks)

2   A girl, **whose** name was Francesca, was walking to school with her mother. As she **passed** the shop she asked her mother if she could **buy** her **some** sweets. Francesca's mother said that **there** was **no** need **for** sweets as she had just eaten a huge bowl of **cereal** covered in sugar **for** breakfast so she wasn't **allowed** sweets. Unfortunately, Francesca did not **hear** her mother as she was **too** excited by the **sight** of a grizzly **bear** that was galloping down the **road**. She tugged at her mother's arm, squealing 'Over **there** Mummy!' She didn't think her mother **would** listen to her, so she **threw** her arms around her mother's knees and the **pair** of them toppled **to** the ground (20 marks)

3   A   On **W**ednesday I am going to the cinema with Rory, Adam and Sam.
4   B   The children from Millbank **S**chool are going on a trip to France next April.
5   C   Mary Ford, whose birthday is next Friday, is my best friend.
6   B   "Please put out the rubbish, Paul," said his mother, as she took another chocolate.
7   C   We are going to London to see Buckingham Palace, the Science Museum and Tower Bridge.
8   N
9   A   My brother and I love to watch nature programmes such as *Springwatch* and *The Blue Planet*.
10 E   We must do the shopping, clean the car, mow the lawn and bake a cake.
11 D   John has many pets, including four cats, two dogs, twelve goldfish and an ancient parrot.
12 N
13 (a) "Where is your homework?" asked Mrs Danes, the maths teacher. (Award 2 marks for a perfect answer, 1 mark if there is only one mistake.)
    (b) "I think I've left it at home," replied Luke. (Award 2 marks for a perfect answer, 1 mark if there is only one mistake.)
    (c) "That," shouted Mrs Danes, "is the excuse you used last week and quite frankly I don't believe it." (Award 2 marks for a perfect answer, 1 mark if there is only one mistake.)
    (d) Looking severely at Luke, Mrs Danes said, "See me at playtime and don't be late." (Award 2 marks for a perfect answer, 1 mark if there is only one mistake.)
    (e) "Yes, Miss," replied Luke. (Award 2 marks for a perfect answer, 1 mark if there is only one mistake.)
    (f) Then, under his breath, he muttered, "You miserable old trout." (Award 2 marks for a perfect answer, 1 mark if there is only one mistake.)

14 My cat Nigel (there's a story behind the name but I'll tell you that another time) lived until the age of eighteen. He was a remarkable cat: he went blind at the age of two but somehow managed to cope with life very well indeed by using his other senses.
    He could find his food by smelling for it and, because he remembered that the cat-flap was just to the left of his food bowl, he could easily find his way to the garden. Once there, he felt his way to the lawn and would then run really fast to the end. Once or twice he forgot where the end was and crashed into the flowerbed but luckily he was not hurt. (19 marks – take 1 mark off for each mistake.) (Note that dashes could be used instead of brackets.)

15 '**Mum**, where's my **bag**?' shouted **David**. (1 mark each)
16 Everyone **going** on the school trip must **bring** a packed lunch. (1 mark each)
17 He ran quickly across the **crowded** classroom and nearly tripped over a **huge** bag. (1 mark each)
18 Things were going **badly** for Simon. He had **carelessly** left his homework in his dad's car. (1 mark each)
19 Megan told **her** a joke but **she** didn't laugh. (1 mark each)
20 I thought the film started at 7, **but** when I got to the cinema I found it didn't begin until eight. (1 mark)
21 I waited **outside** the supermarket **next** to the trolleys where Mum would meet me after she had done the shopping.   (2 prepositions) (1 mark each)
22 The work was so hard that **he/she** had to ask his teacher to help **him/her**. (1 mark each)
23 Alan **ran** quickly so that he would be on time. (1 mark)
24 I like tennis **but/although/whereas** he prefers football. (1 mark)
25 **Even though he had done little practice**, Lloyd played very well. (1 mark)
26 **Ugh!** That tastes disgusting! (1 mark)
27 Last **week** I visited my new senior school. I will be starting school **there** in September. The **building** is brand **new** and the sports hall is **quite modern too**. There **were** lots of amazing **facilities** and I will be **learning** lots of **different** subjects at my new school, including Spanish, Food **Technology**, Japanese and Economics. **Many of** my **friends** from junior school are going to the same school as me in the **autumn** and **we're** all feeling very **excited** about it. Before my visit last week I **had** lots of questions that I wanted to find out the answers to. How many pupils would there be in my class**?** **W**ould the teachers all be **women** like they are at my junior school? Would I have **hours** of homework **every** night? Luckily I had the chance to ask all these questions when I was being shown round by **one** of the **current** Year 7 pupils. He was really friendly and **helpful** and he didn't make me feel stupid for asking. He said that he was very **nervous** before he became a pupil **there** but once he had been at the school **for** a few days he felt like he'd **always** been there. **He** said that the teachers **weren't too** strict and that there wasn't even much homework for the first half term. Now that I **know** a bit more about what to expect I'm really looking **forward** to starting my new school. In fact I think it's going to be amazing! (1 mark each)

2 Reading

Identifying text types (page 43)

<u>Train</u>

1 Answers will vary.
2 Answers will vary.
3 Answers will vary but should include direct speech punctuated properly. For example,
   Anna sprinted back from school to tell her mum the good news.
   "Mum! Mum!" she hollered.
   "What is it?" her mum replied. "Is everything alright?"
   Anna couldn't control her excitement. "I've got some amazing news!" she uttered as she approached her mother, waving a piece of paper in front of her.
   "What exciting news?" asked her mum.
4 Answers will vary.
5 Answers will vary.
6 Answers will vary.
7 Answers will vary.
8 Answers will vary but should include a balance of arguments for and against the topic.
9 Answers will vary.
10 Answers will vary.

Using strategies for tackling comprehension questions (page 54)

<u>Train</u>

1 (a) **How many** children are waiting on the platform?
  (b) **What colour** is the rabbit that escapes from the hutch?
  (c) In line 7, **which word** shows Mr Philips is angry?
  (d) Find **three things that prove** that this passage is set in Victorian times.
  (e) Explain **the meaning of the word** 'tentative' in your own words.
  (f) **How do we know** that Mrs Moody is not a very clever person? **Give evidence from the text** to support your answer.

Understanding the purpose, audience and structure of texts (page 56)

<u>Train</u>

1 Reporting what has happened
  Discussing whether children spend too much time in front of screens
  Persuading people to take up ice-skating

<u>Test</u>

2 It has children as characters, the sentences are simple in structure and the vocabulary is simple. The topic is going to the park, which is a children's activity. It contains colour words.   (3 marks – one for each reason up to 3)

3 Numbered steps, specific details (Gas Mark 4, 20 minutes), imperative verbs.   (1 mark for each reason up to 3)

4 The purpose of this text is to persuade people to exercise (1 mark). It has persuasive sentence starters ('everyone knows'), it uses rhetorical questions, it appeals directly to the reader ('you') and it uses lists of three. (Up to 3 further marks for three reasons)

Summarising key ideas (page 58)

<u>Train</u>

1 Paragraph 1: Charlie arrives at Le Havre on a ship. Paragraph 2: Major tells Lionboy to get to work. Paragraph 3: Charlie notices a crane and some chains swinging near the mast. Paragraph 4: The mast breaks off and is hanging in the air. Paragraph 5: Charlie asks what is happening. Paragraph 6: Charlie is told to stay away from the swaying mast.
2 Paragraph 1: Summary of the trip. Paragraph 2: Children in Portsmouth, teacher scared of heights. Paragraph 3: Tudor day followed by a beach trip. Paragraph 4: Pond-dipping and how they felt about the trip.

<u>Test</u>

3 He had largely enjoyed it. He hadn't realised that he had missed land until he got back.   (1 mark for each key point)
4 The trip was a great success as many fun activities were enjoyed by the children.   (1 mark for each key point)

Using clues to find definitions (page 60)

<u>Train</u>

1 siege: attack by blocking entry and exit to a town or city
  elated: very happy

assemble: gather
mustering: coming together in large numbers
prodigious: very large
revelled: enjoyed themselves

2 (a) <u>dis</u>assemble
 (b) <u>pre</u>determine
 (c) <u>contra</u>indicate
 (d) <u>un</u>accustom<u>ed</u>
 (e) <u>un</u>chang<u>eable</u>

Test

3 plethora: wide variety   (1 mark)
4 resplendent: attractive and colourful   (1 mark)
5 formidable: frightening/inspiring respect   (1 mark)
6 florid: bright/vivid   (1 mark)
7 undulated: moved up and down in waves   (1 mark)

Retrieving specific information in fiction and non-fiction texts (page 62)

Train

1 (a) Ellie had gone into the church because her feet were hurting.
 (b) In the passage it is summertime. (Accept 'summer' but not 'June'.)
 (c) Ellie and Sigrid had set out from Vienna.
 (d) The women went to the mountains on the last Sunday of each month. (Full answer required, not just 'Sunday')
 (e) The women had salami sandwiches and plum cake in their rucksacks. (All details required)
 (f) Any two of the following: The women did cleaning, cooking, shopping and scrubbing for their employers.

Test

2 Answers will vary but should not repeat the words in the passage. (1 mark for each idea successfully reworded up to a maximum of 4.)

Using inference and deduction (page 64)

Train

1 (a) Spring: cut grass, flowers blossoming, baby birds
 (b) Yes: 'breathed in deeply and smiled', 'sketchbook', 'marvelled at the nature'

Test

2 (a) The patchwork is the pattern of bruises on his body.   (1 mark)
 (b) Adventure story or thriller would be sensible options – adventure story on account of the key in his hand and thriller because he has been injured and possibly abandoned on an island. (1 mark for the type of story and 1 mark for the piece of evidence)
 (c) Sanjit is feeling confused/worried. He asks lots of questions, for example, 'How had he arrived here?', 'where was he?' This shows that he doesn't know anything about what has happened to him, which would be very confusing and worrying. He is also injured so that would be worrying as well. (1 mark for the main point and 2 further marks for evidence and explanation)

Making predictions (page 67)

Train

1 A – 5, B – 3, C – 2, D – 1, E – 4

Test

2 1 mark for reference to any of the exotic animals in the text. For example, sharks, crocodiles, dolphins, pet giraffe.
3 Adventure genre needs to be identified for 1 mark, plus 1 mark allocated to each piece of evidence provided up to a maximum of 2 marks. Evidence could include:
 • reference to previous problems with sharks
 • speaking about being attacked by a crocodile
 • possibility of not seeing family again is mentioned
 • children are stranded on an island on their own
 • children have been rescued by dolphins
 • possibility of an adventure on the island is hinted at in the last paragraph.
4 Award 1 mark for each relevant prediction made, up to a total of 6 marks. Prediction could include points such as:
 • Martine will have a wash.
 • Martine and Ben will survive their ordeal.

- Martine will see her grandmother and her giraffe again.
- Ben will help Martine to get home.
- Ben and Martine will come up with a plan to get off the island.
- Ben will see his parents again.
- Ben and Martine will find something interesting on the island.
- Ben and Martine will realise why the dolphins took them to the island.

Separating fact and opinion in non-fiction texts (page 69)

Train

1 (a) Opinion: **Most people believe** that smoking should be illegal.
  (b) Fact: The **Office for National Statistics reported** that in 2014, crime fell by 8 per cent.
  (c) Opinion: It was the **view of the residents** that the new road would cause more pollution.
  (d) Opinion: **Experts suspect** that a cure will be found soon.
2 In this copy of the passage, the facts are identified in **bold** and the opinions are in normal type.

A baby girl had a very lucky escape after **falling 250ft down a ravine in the back of a runaway four-wheel-drive vehicle in France.**

Brian Thompson, 38, and his wife Barbara, 35, had stopped to take photographs next to the Pont de Terenez suspension bridge near Crozon in Brittany when their Nissan Qashqai sped, out of control, down an embankment with their three-month-old daughter, Lucinda, in the child-safety seat.

Mr Thompson, a teacher from Southfield, North-east London, said: "I was sure that she would not have survived the fall. We both were. It was the most terrifying experience of my life."

Miraculously, **Lucinda escaped with just a couple of scratches on her face and a bruised right arm.** "When **I looked through the window and saw her looking at me,** I don't mind admitting that **I burst into tears.** It was a miracle," **said Mr Thompson.**

The vehicle, which was written off in the accident, came to a halt just inches away from a fast-flowing river and had smoke pouring from the engine.

An investigation is now underway into what went wrong. Mr Thompson said, "The handbrake was on when the Qashqai was at the top of the ravine, and it was still on when it was at the bottom."

Doctors have told Lucinda's mother, Barbara, a civil servant, that it will take her daughter several weeks to recover fully from the shock of the accident.

Earlier that day, Mr and Mrs Thompson had called into a local church to light a candle. Mrs Thompson said: "Going into that church was a blessing. **My mother often used to tell me that I should light a candle whenever I visit a church.** The angels must have been watching over my daughter today."

Test

3 These words tell us that Mr Thompson can't quite believe that his daughter survived and he thinks that God must have been involved in saving her. (1 mark) This shows that he may have religious beliefs. (1 mark)
4 Answers will vary. For example: When Mr and Mrs Thomson approached the car they did not expect their daughter to have survived. (1 mark) They were both very afraid of what they would find when they reached the vehicle. (1 mark)
5 The article does give a balanced view of what happened. (1 mark) The article consists mainly of facts although there are some biased views given in the form of quotations from the parents. (1 mark) We learn a lot of information about who, what, where and when the events happened and far less about 'why' or 'how' things happened, which are often not based in fact. (1 mark)

Analysing language (page 71)

Train

1 Answers will vary.
2 Uncle Ralph seems smart and neatly dressed, with clothes that 'blended beautifully with the darker foxiness of Uncle Ralph's hair'. He is also friendly as he 'smiled at him like sunlight on an autumn forest'. The repeated references to a fox suggest he may be clever or cunning.
3 Answers will vary. For example:
In this passage the author creates an atmosphere of extreme fear and helplessness. The language that he has used shows us that the main character is incredibly frightened even though the author does not specifically say that. In the first sentence, the author refers to 'terrors', which makes us think that the passage will not be a happy one. He then makes several references to 'dark' or 'darkness', which makes it seem scary as the character cannot see anything around him. He also uses repetition, saying that he is 'alone' so the reader is aware that there is no one there to

help him. When he introduces sharks, the reader feels afraid because sharks are often considered to be frightening and then he uses the verb 'homing in' which makes the character seem like a target. The author uses lots of short sentences to build tension and make the reader feel afraid, for example, 'I would be eaten alive'. The image of being eaten alive is very frightening, as is the image of drowning slowly. The whole passage gives a sense that there is 'no hope' for the character, especially when he says 'Nothing could save me'. In the last paragraph the adverb and adjective give a terrifying mood to the piece. The author writes 'frantically' and 'impenetrable' which make the character seem panicked and in a desperate situation. Finally the last, short sentence, with the repetition of the word 'nothing' makes the whole situation seem utterly hopeless.

4   Personification to make the forest seem part of the action: 'the trees tensed to listen' (the word 'Forest' also uses a capital to make it appear to be a proper noun). Verbs for effect, such as 'crisped' to indicate how his skin felt, as if the fever was burning him.

Test

5   The metaphor 'this jungle of moss' makes the garden seem a dangerous place.   (1 mark)
6   Award 1 mark for example and 1 mark for explanation. Answer could include:
     'The sharp-seeming grass blades, waist high' – if the grass is up to her waist she must be tiny.
     'she held the flower, like a parasol' – if a primrose seems as big as a parasol the girl must be very small.
7   Award 1 mark for each example (up to 2 marks) and 1 mark for each explanation (up to 2 marks). Answers could include:
     'Jungle of moss' – this makes it clear that the girl is small as the garden seems like a dangerous place.
     'If she pressed the leaf these rolled like marbles' – this shows how close the girl is to the dewdrops and how big they look. It also reminds us that the character is a child as she compares them to a toy.
     'when she held the flower, like a parasol' – this makes the garden seem like a pleasant place to be, in contrast to the jungle earlier on. This may mean that the girl is more comfortable being there.
     'It curled immediately and became a ball' – again this reminds us that the character is a child. She wants someone to play with her, so she compares lots of the things around her to games or toys.

Test 2: Fiction comprehension (page 76)

1   It was cold and foggy.   (1 mark)
2   Award 3 marks for any sensible answer that includes three of the following points: The author has created a sinister atmosphere in the opening paragraphs. She refers to a storm that has just passed and the little girl shivering, which make the passage seem spooky. She also says that the cold is very unpleasant, using the phrase 'heart-dragging', which makes the scene seem sinister as it is an unusual, scary image.   (3 marks)
3   Award 2 marks for any sensible answer that includes two of the following points: The phrase 'skeletal branches of the trees' reminds the reader that it is winter, so the branches are bare, which makes them look like bones, but it also creates an eerie and frightening atmosphere because skeletons are often associated with being scary.   (2 marks)
4   Answer should explain that Teo is scared or shocked when she sees a large white eel in the water (1 mark). When it winks at her she realises that it is a vampire eel (1 mark), which means that Bajamonte Tiepolo is back so she needs to tell her friends and they need to do something about it (1 mark).   (3 marks)
5   Two points needed for 2 marks. The nurse uses the word 'Ma'am' very often when she is addressing the Queen. This shows that she respects her as it is a polite way to speak. The nurse is also very gentle in the way that she speaks to the Queen. (2 marks)
6   Award 1 mark for an explanation of how it makes the reader feel and 1 mark for evidence or explanation. For example: The appearance of the cormorant makes the reader feel uncomfortable. It is described as a 'shadow' with 'ink-black wings', which make it seem sinister and frightening.   (2 marks)
7   The phrase 'the teaspoon still clutched in her tiny, wrinkled hand' makes the Queen seem vulnerable.   (1 mark)
8   Ideally two comments about Teo's character should be made, with two separate pieces of evidence to support them. Award any sensible answer, for example:
     Teo seems to be a sad girl. We know this because the author says that she feels hopeless and she trudges home.
     Teo also seems to blame herself for something bad that has happened. She seems quite hard on herself as she says that she is to blame for Bajamonte Tiepolo's return.   (4 marks)
9   crystalline – clear like a crystal; embedded – fixed in; pinafore – apron; uncannily – surprisingly.   (4 marks)
10   C (1 mark)
11   E (1 mark)
12   A (1 mark)
13   D (1 mark)
14   C (1 mark)
15   B (1 mark)

Test 3: Non-fiction comprehension (page 79)

1   The narrator was worried because all of the hotels and lodgings seemed to be closed and he didn't know where he would stay.   (1 mark)
2   The narrator likes/is fond of Britain. He likens walking through the streets to being in a *Bulldog Drummond* film and he thinks it is 'rather wonderful' to have an English town to himself. (Award 1 mark for what he thinks and 1 mark for a piece of evidence.)   (2 marks)

3   Any two points for 2 marks: The narrator seems clumsy because he trips over the step. He hits his face on the door. He knocks over lots of milk bottles. (2 marks)

4   Award 1 mark for each part of the answer. The phrase 'on the front' means 'on the seafront'. This is confusing for the narrator as he is American and so he is not familiar with the words/he would use a different word to describe the seafront. (2 marks)

5   Award marks for any sensible answer containing any four of the following points: The narrator is expecting the hotel owner to be friendly. We know this because he refers to a 'kindly owner' and he expects to have a 'cheery conversation' and to be offered food. In reality the owner is very unfriendly. She speaks in very short sentences and uses a 'sharp voice'. She does not let him in or make him any food and then she slams a window when he is asking her a question.   (4 marks)

6   Award 1 mark for identifying that the narrator did not enjoy his experience at the French hotel. Award the remaining 3 marks for relevant evidence and explanation: His stay at the hotel had cost a lot of money. We know this because it says he handed over 'an exceptionally plump wad' of francs. He also refers to the hotelier as 'beady-eyed', which makes him seem unpleasant and he refers to the bed as 'lumpy' which suggests it wasn't comfortable.   (4 marks)

7   The narrator dreams about the Arctic because he is very cold sitting on the bench on the seafront (1 mark) and the Arctic is a very cold place (1 mark). (2 marks)

8   Award 2 marks for two of the following points. The narrator is not comfortable or happy about sleeping outside but he thinks it is his only choice. (1 mark) He also finds it impossible to get comfortable on the bench as he says 'that made reclining in comfort an impossibility'. (1 mark) He is also too cold to appreciate how beautiful the scenery is (1 mark). (2 marks)

9   The author uses the phrase 'death's sweet kiss' because he is so cold and uncomfortable (1 mark) that he thinks that death would be more pleasant than what he is experiencing at the moment (1 mark). (2 marks)

10   D (1 mark)

11   C (1 mark)

12   D (1 mark)

13   B (1 mark)

14   E (1 mark)

15   C (1 mark)

Test 4: Poetry comprehension (page 82)

Train

1   The sun rises on the left side of the ship. (1 mark)

2   'Red as a rose is she' (1 mark) The author chose this because roses are associated with love and beauty. It may refer to the colour of her cheeks or her lips. (2 marks)

3   The wedding guest is listening to the mariner's story. (1 mark)

4   The weather turns cold. (1 mark) There is mist and snow. (1 mark) There are huge green icebergs floating next to the ship. (1 mark)

5   Any two of the following: cracked, growled, roared, howled (Modern English spelling required for the marks.)   (2 marks)

6   The wedding guest interrupts the mariner because of the look on the mariner's face. (2 marks for an answer conveying this point)

7   C (1 mark)

8   The poet uses personification (1 mark) to suggest that the storm is strong and evil (tyrannous). (1 mark) The poet also suggests that the storm has wings like a bird that is chasing them. (1 mark)

9   The person who steers the ship. (Do not accept just 'member of the crew'.) (1 mark)

10   A (1 mark)

11   B (1 mark)

12   The poet describes the size of the ice (1 mark) – 'mast-high' (1 mark). He describes it making noises like an animal (1 mark) – 'It crack'd and growl'd, and roar'd and howl'd'. (1 mark)

Chapter 3: Composition

Choosing a task (page 87)

Train

1   Answers will vary but should include a range of up to five ideas of different interpretations covering a variety of text types.
   (a) The Supermarket – a story, a newspaper article, a description, etc.
   (b) Friendship – a balanced argument (everybody needs friends), a short story, a diary entry, etc.
   (c) A time when you were treated unfairly – this suggests a personal response piece but could be in a diary or recount format. Ideas should include different times, situations or people that were unfair.

Planning (page 89)

Train

1 Answers will vary but should show a clear beginning, middle and end and adhere to the given criteria.
2 Answers will vary but should show a clear beginning, middle and end and adhere to the given criteria.
3 Answers will vary but should show a clear beginning, middle and end and adhere to the given criteria.

Test

4 Use the relevant success grid (pages 141–144) to award a mark out of 25.

Narrative writing from a title (page 92)

Train

1 Answers will vary but must adhere closely to the title given. Ideas may vary between narrative genres, should be original and interesting and should be planned with a clear beginning, middle and end.

Responding to textual prompts (page 93)

Train

1 Answers will vary but the entire plan must centre around the use of the given phrase. It should not appear as an afterthought. For example, the thing that 'vanished' should be central to the story throughout. It must be a thing as it says 'it' vanished rather than 'he' or 'she'.
2 Answers will vary but the entire plan must centre around the use of the given quote. It should not appear as an afterthought. For example, if a character says those words, it must be linked to the main theme of the plot.
3 Answers will vary.
   (a) The 'it' in the given line must be an 'it' rather than a person. The plan must be for a short story and should include a clear beginning, middle and end. The sentence lends itself well to sci-fi or fantasy but any other original and engaging interpretation is allowed.
   (b) The short story plan should be clear and exciting. The letter could be a letter in an envelope or a letter of the alphabet. It could get lost during the story or be lost at the start.
   (c) A variety of genres could be used here – narrative, discursive, diary, etc. This task lends itself to some thought-ful writing on what it means to be brave or a story with a clear moral based on courage. Plans should be clearly centred on the theme and originality should be rewarded.

Test

4 Use the relevant success grid (for narrative writing, personal response, letters, responding to pictures and textual prompts, page 141) to award a mark out of 25.

Responding to pictures (page 95)

Train

1 Answers will vary but the two plans should differ from one another. Original and unusual interpretations should be credited but each plan should be clearly linked to the picture.
2 Answers will vary but the two plans should differ from one another. Original and unusual interpretations should be credited but each plan should be clearly linked to the picture.
3 Answers will vary but the two plans should differ from one another; one of them should be fiction and the other non-fiction. Original and unusual interpretations should be credited but each plan should be clearly linked to the picture.

Test

4 Use the relevant success grid (for narrative writing, personal response, letters, responding to pictures and textual prompts, page 141) to award a mark out of 25.

Continuation (page 97)

Train

1 (a) The characters are exhausted and seem to be escaping some kind of danger. They are relieved to be at the top of the hill and they seem to know each other quite well.
   (b) It is a hillside; it is misty and the conditions seem to be unpleasant.
   (c) There is a balance of dialogue and narration, some description and the dialogue is used to tell more of the story.
   (d) William's final words suggest that whatever they are running away from has followed them, or that a new danger has emerged.
2 Plans will vary but should feature the points made above.

Test

3 Use the relevant success grid (for continuing a story, page 142) to award a mark out of 25.

Book review (page 99)

<u>Train</u>

1 (a) Answers will vary but the plan should have a considerable amount devoted to the humorous elements of the book, with examples.
   (b) Answers will vary but the plan should have a considerable amount devoted to why the book was so memorable, with examples.
   (c) Answers will vary but the plan should cover the key features of the book: plot, characters, setting and personal response.

<u>Test</u>

2 Use the relevant success grid (for writing about a book you have read, page 143) to award a mark out of 25.

Personal response (page 101)

<u>Train</u>

1 (a) Write about a time when you needed to be **brave**.
   (b) Describe the most **memorable** day of your life.
   (c) Write about the most **spectacular** place you have ever visited.
   (d) Write about a **challenge** you have faced.
   (e) Describe a time when you felt **disappointed**.
2 Answers will vary, but might include some of the following ideas:
   (a) This could be a first performance, first day at school, trying something for the first time, having a difficult conversation, etc.
   (b) This might be winning something, meeting a friend for the first time, an amazing birthday, etc.
   (c) This could be anywhere, home or abroad.
   (d) This could be learning something new, exams, facing a fear, etc.
   (e) This could be having an argument, failing an exam, not getting picked for a team, etc.
3 Answers will vary.

<u>Test</u>

4 Use the relevant success grid (for narrative writing, personal response, letters, responding to pictures and textual prompts, page 141) to award a mark out of 25.

Discursive and persuasive writing (page 103)

<u>Train</u>

1 (a) discursive
   (b) persuasive
   (c) persuasive
   (d) discursive
   (e) persuasive
2 Answers will vary but the plan should be for a persuasive composition.
3 Answers will vary but the plan should be for a persuasive composition.
4 Answers will vary but the plan should be for a persuasive composition.

<u>Test</u>

5 Use the relevant success grid (for discursive and persuasive writing, page 144) to award a mark out of 25.

Starting and ending your writing (page 105)

<u>Train</u>

1 Answers will vary.
2 Answers will vary but should follow the suggestions given for story openings.
3 Use the success grids on pages 141–144.
4 Use the success grids on pages 141–144.
5 Use the success grids on pages 141–144.

<u>Test</u>

6 Use the relevant success grid (for narrative writing, personal response, letters, responding to pictures and textual prompts, page 141) to award a mark out of 25.

Improving your writing: adverbials (page 108)

<u>Train</u>

1 Answers will vary. For example:
   (a) Smiling broadly, she opened the front door.

(b) They watched the fireworks, cheering and laughing.
   (c) After a tricky race, the sprinter reached the finish line.
   (d) Everybody opened their presents before they ate breakfast.
2 Answers will vary. For example:
   (a) As the clock struck two, the doors swung open.
   (b) With a smile on his face, Joel picked up the phone.
   (c) The trolls planned their revenge under the bridge.
   (d) She had homework every other day.

Test

3 Use the relevant success grid (for narrative writing, personal response, letters, responding to pictures and textual prompts, page 141) to award a mark out of 25. Expect to find a considerable range of adverbial phrases and clauses. This will add to the style and grammar scores.

Improving your writing: flashbacks (page 109)

Train

1 Answers will vary. For example:
   (a) She thought harder and the memory started to come back to her.
   (b) Suddenly she caught a glimpse in her mind of how things were before.
   (c) He wondered whether he remembered it correctly.
   (d) Paul couldn't stop thinking about that summer four years ago.
2 Answers will vary. For example:
   (a) Without warning, a loud crash brought her back to the present.
   (b) She was startled back to reality with a jolt.
   (c) The bell rang and his thoughts returned to his current predicament.
   (d) As the light flicked on, Kay's attention turned back to today.

Test

3 Use the relevant success grid (for narrative writing, personal response, letters, responding to pictures and textual prompts, page 141) to award a mark out of 25.

Improving your writing: imagery and descriptive techniques (page 110)

Train

1 Answers will vary but should use a range of techniques as explained. For example: Battalions of trees lined the paths of the luscious park.

Test

2 Use the relevant success grid (for narrative writing, personal response, letters, responding to pictures and textual prompts, page 141) to award a mark out of 25.

Improving your writing: mimicking style (page 112)

Train

1 It is night, the moon is out, the weather is calm, the water is cold.
2 Ben is alone, his mum doesn't know where he is.
3 Lots of description, questions, third person, past tense.
4 Clue that something bad might happen: 'What she didn't know wouldn't hurt her, would it?'

Test

5 Use the relevant success grid (for narrative writing, personal response, letters, responding to pictures and textual prompts, page 141) to award a mark out of 25.

Improving your writing: sentence structure (page 114)

Train

1 Answers will vary but should include improved sentence structures, lengths and starters. There may be some added dialogue.
2 Use the relevant success grid (pages 141–144) to re-mark the new version of the piece of work and compare the two.

Test

3 Use the relevant success grid (for narrative writing, personal response, letters, responding to pictures and textual prompts, page 141) to award a mark out of 25.

Improving your writing: verbs for effect (page 116)

<u>Train</u>

1 Answers will vary. For example:
   (a) She grabbed/cradled/gripped/fondled the mysterious key in her hand.
   (b) She sprinted/zoomed/raced/galloped to the shops. Note that 'quickly' would probably be removed when using one of these verbs.
   (c) He gazed/peeped/stared/glanced at the birds with interest. Note that some verbs require the removal of the word 'at'.
   (d) He created/constructed/designed/assembled a beautiful model of a Viking ship.
   (e) We all enjoyed/relished/delighted in/appreciated the food in the restaurant.
2 Answers will vary. For example:
   (a) jog, trot, dash, scamper, dart, sprint, gallop, race, bound, scramble
   (b) whisper, mumble, utter, state, announce, ask, add, declare, recite, proclaim
   (c) glimpse, glance, gaze, view, examine, notice, watch, observe, regard, spot

<u>Test</u>

3 Use the relevant success grid (for narrative writing, personal response, letters, responding to pictures and textual prompts, page 141) to award a mark out of 25. A range of verbs should be used.

Improving your writing: choosing a point of view (page 117)

<u>Train</u>

1 Answers will vary. For example:
   (a) A particular dwarf, Snow White, Evil Queen, etc.
   (b) Any key character
   (c) The wolf, one of the pigs
   (d) The wolf, Grandma, Red Riding Hood
   (e) Willy Wonka, one of the visiting children, Grandpa Joe, etc.
   (f) The hare, the tortoise, a spectator
2 Answers will vary, but reward interesting or particularly effective choices.

<u>Test</u>

3 Use the relevant success grid (for narrative writing, personal response, letters, responding to pictures and textual prompts, page 141) to award a mark out of 25.

Improving your writing: linking devices (page 118)

<u>Train</u>

1 Answers will vary. For example:
   (a) I know that you are busy, **however** I hope you can find time to read this letter.
   (b) I am only a child, **nevertheless** I believe that young people's opinions should be heard.
   (c) **Obviously**, pollution is a worldwide issue which needs to be addressed.
   (d) **Eventually**, it will be too late to make a change.
   (e) We both know there are changes to be made, **therefore** I ask that you consider my suggestions.

<u>Test</u>

2 Use the relevant success grid (for discursive and persuasive writing, page 144) to award a mark out of 25.

Test 5: Composition (page 120)

Use the relevant success grid to award a mark out of 25.

Test 6: Composition (page 121)

Use the relevant success grid to award a mark out of 25.

11+ Sample tests

Spelling, punctuation and grammar (page 129)

1 B (1 mark)	6 B (1 mark)	11 C (1 mark)	16 B/D (2 marks)	21 A/C (2 marks)
2 C (1 mark)	7 C (1 mark)	12 B (1 mark)	17 A/C (2 marks)	22 A/A (2 marks)
3 C (1 mark)	8 B (1 mark)	13 A (1 mark)	18 C/C (2 marks)	23 A/D (2 marks)
4 C (1 mark)	9 B (1 mark)	14 D (1 mark)	19 A/D (2 marks)	24 B/D (2 marks)
5 B (1 mark)	10 B (1 mark)	15 N (1 mark)	20 A/D (2 marks)	25 A/A (2 marks)

26　Mrs Roberts looked round the classroom and sighed. **Although** she had been a teacher for over thirty years, this class was **different from** any other she had ever **known**. They were the most messy, untidy group of children ever. They had gone out to the playground leaving the classroom looking **as though** a bomb had hit it. Books **lay** on the floor, chairs were overturned, desks were covered with pieces of paper and a school scarf was **hanging from** one of the lights. 'Right,' she said to herself. 'I've **had** enough of this. As soon as they come back I will make them clear **up** this mess. And to stop them doing it again, they can jolly well **remain** in the classroom for the whole of the lunch break and **write** me a letter of apology.'   (10 marks)

27　**W**hen you go to the **theatre** today you expect a roof over your head, warmth, **comfortable** seats and peace and **quiet. In** Shakespeare's day it was not like this at all. If you were not well off you got wet on a rainy day. You would be standing and get jostled by apple-sellers. **Y**ou would chat to your neighbours and hiss or cheer the actors. **Y**ou could look up at those richer than you who sat with a small roof over their heads on dry seats. They in turn looked **enviously** at the noblemen and women who sat above the stage in the best seats of all. **On** stage boy actors took the parts of young girls and older men played the **women,** for not until long after Shakespeare died was it thought proper for **females** to appear on stage.   (1 mark each)

Comprehension 1 (page 132)

Answers are worth 1 mark each.

1	D	8	D	15	E
2	D	9	E	16	B
3	D	10	D	17	D
4	E	11	C	18	B
5	A	12	B	19	A
6	B	13	A	20	D
7	B	14	C		

Comprehension 2 (page 137)

1　(a) This phrase shows us that Humphrey is nervous/afraid/unsure. When we are scared our heart thumps loudly. (1 mark)

(b) This shows us that Humphrey didn't want to be noticed. 'Worming' makes it sound like he is moving silently and trying to sneak up on them and he is cautious as he doesn't want to be caught.   (1 mark)

2　The men were looking forward to it. The fact that they were eager to get there and they didn't want the fight to start without them, saying 'Only let 'em dally till we come' shows this.   (2 marks, 1 mark for how the men were feeling and 1 mark for the evidence)

3　Award marks for any sensible answer that shows engagement with the text. Evidence could include any of the following: 'Humphrey almost fell down the ladder in his eagerness', 'Humphrey was shaking with excitement', 'he could hardly contain himself in silence'. The answer should also clearly include whether they think Humphrey is right or wrong to be eager to join them and a brief explanation of why they think this.   (3 marks)

4　The phrase means 'Don't be too proud/fancy to help us,.   (1 mark)

5　They thought he was a stable lad/someone who worked at the inn. Evidence: We know this because the men expect him to help/call him 'boy'.   (2 marks, 1 mark for the sort of person and 1 mark for the evidence)

6　In order to gain all of the marks, there must be a detailed explanation of the last few paragraphs showing understanding of the following:
• Humphrey is a **fat** young lad who is **looking offended** and **trying to seem important**, which makes him seem amusing to an adult.   (3 marks)

7　Award 1 mark (up to a maximum of 3) for concrete examples such as: 'men-of-war'/'gentry'/'gallants'/travelling on horseback.
Also award marks for examples of old-fashioned language/sentence structures.   (3 marks)

8　There is nothing in the passage to help with this, so answers need to include reasonable possibilities. These could include (but are not restricted to) the fact that he is in Robin's care and probably thinks that Robin would not let him go off to see the ships. Perhaps he is not looking forward to staying with his relations. Perhaps his relations are unkind to him as his cousin calls him a 'stomachy lad', meaning that he is fat.   (3 marks, 1 for each possibility)

9　To gain all of the available marks, the answer must be one paragraph (at least six sentences long) and it must include well-punctuated direct speech. The characters should be consistent with the original text and an attempt should have been made to make the writing sound like it is set in the past. Old-fashioned language is not compulsory, but anything too modern will cost marks. The best answers will convey the attitudes of both Humphrey and the men he is speaking to.   (6 marks)

Composition 1 (page 139)

Use the relevant success grid (pages 141–144) to award a mark out of 25.

Composition 2 (page 140)

Use the relevant success grid (pages 141–144) to award a mark out of 25.